ITBS

Success Strategies

Level 11 Grade 5

ITBS Test Review for the Iowa Tests of Basic Skills

Dear Future Exam Success Story:

Congratulations on your purchase of our study guide. Our goal in writing our study guide was to cover the content on the test, as well as provide insight into typical test taking mistakes and how to overcome them.

Standardized tests are a key component of being successful, which only increases the importance of doing well in the high-pressure high-stakes environment of test day. How well you do on this test will have a significant impact on your future, and we have the research and practical advice to help you execute on test day.

The product you're reading now is designed to exploit weaknesses in the test itself, and help you avoid the most common errors test takers frequently make.

How to use this study guide

We don't want to waste your time. Our study guide is fast-paced and fluff-free. We suggest going through it a number of times, as repetition is an important part of learning new information and concepts.

First, read through the study guide completely to get a feel for the content and organization. Read the general success strategies first, and then proceed to the content sections. Each tip has been carefully selected for its effectiveness.

Second, read through the study guide again, and take notes in the margins and highlight those sections where you may have a particular weakness.

Finally, bring the manual with you on test day and study it before the exam begins.

Your success is our success

We would be delighted to hear about your success. Send us an email and tell us your story. Thanks for your business and we wish you continued success.

Sincerely,

Mometrix Test Preparation Team

TABLE OF CONTENTS

Top 15 Test Taking Tips

1. Know the test directions, duration, topics, question types, how many questions
2. Setup a flexible study schedule at least 3-4 weeks before test day
3. Study during the time of day you are most alert, relaxed, and stress free
4. Maximize your learning style; visual learner use visual study aids, auditory learner use auditory study aids
5. Focus on your weakest knowledge base
6. Find a study partner to review with and help clarify questions
7. Practice, practice, practice
8. Get a good night's sleep; don't try to cram the night before the test
9. Eat a well balanced meal
10. Wear comfortable, loose fitting, layered clothing; prepare for it to be either cold or hot during the test
11. Eliminate the obviously wrong answer choices, then guess the first remaining choice
12. Pace yourself; don't rush, but keep working and move on if you get stuck
13. Maintain a positive attitude even if the test is going poorly
14. Keep your first answer unless you are positive it is wrong
15. Check your work, don't make a careless mistake

Reading

Being able to read well is very important for anyone who wants to succeed in school, and it's also a key factor when it comes to being successful at life in general. When you stop and think about it, it's obvious that good reading skills are essential for success in school. After all, nearly every class and course you take from now until the time you graduate will require you to do some reading in order to do get a high grade. If you think you read a lot for school now, just wait until you get into high school.

If you attend college or university after high school, this skill becomes even more important. Just as high school requires a lot more reading than 5th grade, college and university courses require much more reading than high school classes. In life outside of school, once you're an adult, you'll need to be able to read well for a wide variety of reasons. Also, once you develop good reading skills, they never go away. It's much easier to develop them now than to try to pick them up later, after years of neglecting them.

Practice Test

The exercises in this chapter will help you improve your reading skills. Read each passage, and then answer the questions that follow it.

Living on a Ranch

Marcus Morgan lives in Laramie, Wyoming, with his family. Laramie is between the Snowy Mountain Range and the Laramie Mountain Range, west of Cheyenne, Wyoming.

Marcus and his family own a large cattle ranch outside of the city along U.S. Route 287. The Bar M Bar Ranch raises both beef and dairy cattle, along with a small herd of sheep. Mrs. Morgan keeps chickens and raises a small garden to feed the family. Marcus and his two brothers, James and Robert, have to help with chores and taking care of the animals.

Life starts early on the ranch. Mrs. Morgan rings the bell to bring everyone in for breakfast at 4:30 am. The family eats breakfast with the ranch hands, and then the boys do their morning chores before heading off to school. When the boys return from school, they have more chores to complete before dinner and time for homework.

Everyone has a job on a ranch. Mr. Morgan supervises the ranch hands, oversees repairs, and takes care of all the vehicles on the ranch. Mrs. Morgan is in charge of paying the bills and making sure everyone is fed. Marcus, at 15 years old, is the oldest child and has the most responsibility. He has to let the sheep out every morning and bring them back in every evening. He helps in the milking barn or with branding beef cattle when needed. He also takes care of the working dogs used all over the ranch. James gathers eggs, brings in a fresh pail of milk every morning, and cleans out horse stalls in the evenings. Robert, the baby of the family, helps his mom around the house and in the garden.

Marcus especially likes working with the sheep. In the mornings, he and his favorite working dog, Shep, run the sheep out of their corral into the big pasture so they can graze. Marcus uses whistles and calls to tell Shep where he wants the sheep to go, and Shep herds them. In the evenings, Marcus and Shep round up the sheep from the pasture and return them to the corral. Then Marcus must feed the sheep and check them all for injuries. In the spring, Marcus and Shep help Mr. Morgan bring the sheep into the shearing shed one at a time to have their wool sheared.

1. Where is the Bar M Bar Ranch?
   a. Cheyenne, Wyoming
   b. The Snowy Mountains
   c. Laramie, Wyoming
   d. The Laramie Mountains

2. How does Marcus tell Shep what to do?
   a. Marcus uses a clicker in his hand.
   b. Marcus uses a leash.
   c. Marcus lets Shep do all the work alone.
   d. Marcus uses whistles and calls.

3. Which of the following choices best summarizes the fifth paragraph?
   a. Marcus and Shep take care of the sheep.
   b. Marcus enjoys working with the sheep.
   c. Shep is a good sheep dog.
   d. Mr. Morgan sheers the sheep in the spring.

4. From this passage, you can tell that:
   a. Everyone has a job on a ranch.
   b. Children work much harder than adults on the ranch.
   c. Living on a ranch is no fun.
   d. Marcus does not enjoy his chores.

5. Mr. Morgan supervises the ranch hands and the outside chores. Which of the following choices best describes Mrs. Morgan's chores?
   a. She is in charge of the sheep.
   b. She is in charge of the chickens.
   c. She is in charge of the household and bills.
   d. She is in charge of the children.

6. From the passage, the reader can tell:
   a. Ten ranch hands work on the Bar M Bar Ranch.
   b. Working and living on a ranch is a full time job.
   c. A ranch in Wyoming is a lonely place.
   d. Mr. Morgan doesn't like sheep.

7. From this passage, the phrase "ranch hands" most likely means:
   a. The hands of people who work on the ranch.
   b. People who work on a ranch owned by someone else.
   c. The machines used to milk dairy cattle.
   d. A way to repair a fence.

8. Marcus, James, and Robert are different ages, but they have something in common in this passage. Which sentence best describes what they have in common?
   a. They all help with chores on the ranch.
   b. They all take care of the working dogs.
   c. They all have brown hair.
   d. They all have to shear sheep.

Geocaching

"Would you like to go geocaching with me this weekend, Tommy?" asked his father. "I have found a couple of new ones near the creek that I think would be fun. We could invite your friend Sam to join us."

"Sure, Dad. I love geocaching," said Tommy. "Should we go Saturday?" They agreed that they would leave Saturday morning to find the new geocaches, and Tommy ran to call Sam and invite him. Sam agreed to come with them. Although he wasn't sure what geocaching was, he always had fun with Tommy and his dad.

Friday night, Tommy and his dad got their gear ready. Both of them had handheld GPS units, hiking boots with good wool socks, a backpack to carry first aid gear, water, and swag for the cache such as plastic soldiers, a water pistol, and some playing cards.

Tommy's father made sure that they had a compass and a map, bug spray, and hats, and he printed out the coordinates for the geocaches. Tommy had given Sam a list of things to bring with him, as well.

Saturday morning, Tommy and Dad picked up Sam at his house and off they went. "Mr. Jones, could you explain to me what geocaching is?" Sam asked, as they were getting in the car.

"Of course, Sam. Basically, it's like a giant worldwide treasure hunt. People hide geocaches, or containers, then take the coordinates with their GPS and enter the coordinates into a website where people like us can find them. Then other people, like us, go hunting for these containers. Some of them are very tiny, just big enough to have a piece of paper for the date and your name. Some of them are large enough to hold books or toys and a logbook. Sometimes, people even put disposable cameras in them so you can take a picture of yourself at the cache. Sometimes, there are even items in the cache that can be tracked, so you can see how they move around the world."

Tommy's dad could see that Sam was still a little confused, but he knew that the boy would catch on as they got going. Mr. Jones put the coordinates for the first cache into his GPS, and off they went. "It looks like this first cache is only two miles from here," he told the boys.

The GPS led the trio to a small parking area just inside the local park, where they stopped and got their backpacks on, sprayed themselves with bug spray, and reset the GPS for off-road walking. "It looks like we have about 400 feet to go just that way," Mr. Jones said, as they headed away from the car into the woods. When they arrived at the location, Sam looked around. "I don't see anything," he complained.

Tommy laughed. "Our GPS is accurate to 15 feet, Sam, which means that the cache container is within 15 feet of Dad right now, but in any direction. The way we do it is Dad stands still, and I walk 15 feet from him. Then we know how far in each direction to look. Why don't I walk 15 feet to his right and you go left? Then we know exactly where to search." Sam agreed, and the boys quickly marked off their search area. "The cache is medium sized, Sam, so be looking for something like the plastic boxes your mom puts leftovers in, okay?"

Tommy, Sam, and Mr. Jones searched for about 10 minutes. They looked in tree branches, under rocks and leaves, and even inside of a hollow log before Sam yelled, "I think I found it!" Sure enough, he had found the container under a pile of leaves beside the hollow log. Since this was Sam's first find, Tommy and his dad let Sam open the box and choose an item to trade. Sam chose to take a bouncy rubber ball and leave a water gun. Mr. Jones signed the logbook for all of them, and they hid the cache back where they found it. "That was so much fun, Tommy! I'm so glad you asked me to come along," Sam said excitedly.

"Does that mean you boys are ready to find the next one?" Mr. Jones asked. The boys cheered and the three set off for the car.

1. Why did Sam go with Tommy and Mr. Jones?
    a. He loved geocaching.
    b. Tommy offered to give him a water pistol.
    c. He always had fun when he was with Tommy and Mr. Jones.
    d. He wanted to go swimming in the creek.

2. Why did Sam and Tommy have to mark off a search area?
    a. The GPS was accurate only to 15 feet.
    b. Tommy's dad wanted to make the boys work harder.
    c. Searching a big area was more fun.
    d. Tommy wanted Sam to learn how to search.

3. Tommy gave Sam a list of items to bring with him. What might have been on that list?
    a. A towel, a beach ball, and a sand bucket
    b. A raincoat, an umbrella, and rubber boots
    c. Wool socks, hiking boots, and a backpack
    d. Books, a flashlight, and a tent

4. Which of the following sentences is the best summary of paragraph five?
   a. Geocaching is a treasure hunt for small containers using GPS coordinates.
   b. Geocaching is a game for people to play online.
   c. Geocaching is about logbooks and taking pictures.
   d. Geocaching is something only boys do.

5. From the passage, "swag" most likely means
   a. How a person walks
   b. Small items or toys to trade
   c. A bag with money in it
   d. A backpack to carry your gear in

6. In the car, Mr. Jones teaches Sam about geocaching. Does Tommy teach Sam anything?
   a. Yes, Tommy teaches Sam about using a backpack.
   b. No, Sam teaches Tommy about comic books.
   c. No, Mr. Jones teaches Sam about drawing on a map.
   d. Yes, Tommy teaches Sam about marking off a search area.

7. This story is about:
   a. Two friends going into the woods for an adventure
   b. Two friends going geocaching with Mr. Jones
   c. Tommy teaching Sam about searching
   d. Sam learning how to use a GPS

8. From clues in the story, "cache" most likely means:
   a. A hollow log
   b. A path through the woods
   c. A pirate's treasure
   d. A hiding place

Dance Class

Jillian and Samantha attend dance classes at Ms. Suzie's Dance Studio every Friday after school. The twins have matching leotards and tights. They both wear their long brown hair up in a bun. However, that's all they have in common at Ms. Suzie's.

Jillian loves classical dance and is taking a ballet class. After she went into the classroom, she put on her satin slippers and began to stretch her legs at the *barre*. Jillian watches herself in the wall-length mirrors to make sure her feet are moving correctly on the wooden floor. When Ms. Suzie turns on the music, Jillian and the other ballerinas get into line and settle into position one. Jillian stood with the balls of her feet completely turned out, her heels touching and her feet forming a straight line. As Ms. Suzie took the class through the other four positions, Jillian thought about what was coming up later. Ms. Suzie had promised that today they would start learning *en pointe*. "*En pointe*" is French for "on the tip," when ballerinas stand on the tip of their toes as they dance. Jillian brought special toe shoes with her today, reinforced to support her feet and protect her toes.

In another classroom, Samantha slipped into her tap shoes and began to warm up on the wooden floor. Tap shoes are like dress shoes with little metal plates under the toes and the heels. The plates are attached by small screws that can be loosened to change the sound of the tapping. Ms. Jessica, one of Ms. Suzie's dance instructors, started the music. Samantha and her friends started working on their tap steps, watching themselves in the mirrors on the wall. Samantha started with basic tap steps, called single steps, and quickly moved through the different steps like the brush, the shuffle, and the ball change. Samantha likes the modern movements and music of tap. Jillian and Samantha both are practicing with extra effort. The school recital is next week, and they want to do their very best. The recital was so important to them that last month, their dad built a mini dance studio in the basement. It has a wooden floor, mirrors, and a *barre*. There is only room enough for one of them to practice at a time, so they take turns in the mini studio. Jillian practices in the mornings and Samantha in the evenings. They are really ready for the big night.

After class, the girls walked home together excitedly talking about their classes.

1. Why do Jillian and Samantha go to Ms. Suzie's?
    a. They want to learn to dance.
    b. They want to learn how to dress alike.
    c. Jillian talked Samantha into taking a ballet class.
    d. They just pass by on their way home.

2. Although they are dressed alike, the girls are very different. What is the big difference between them?
    a. Jillian has blonde hair, while Samantha's is brown.
    b. Samantha is wearing shorts, but Jillian is wearing a leotard.
    c. Jillian loves ballet, and Samantha loves tap.
    d. Samantha walks home, and Jillian takes the bus.

3. Ms. Suzie and Ms. Jessica both teach dance classes in studios. What did the two classrooms have in common?
    a. Both classrooms have TV's and game machines in them.
    b. Both classrooms have shoe cubbies and rugs.
    c. Both classrooms have wood walls and carpets.
    d. Both classrooms have wooden floors and mirrors.

4. According to the passage, ballet is:
    a. Only for girls
    b. Only for boys
    c. A classical type of dance
    d. A modern type of dance

5. A "*barre*" is:
    a. A bar of soap in the dish
    b. A bar of light through a window
    c. A bar of chocolate to eat after class
    d. A bar on the wall for stretching

6. This story mostly is about:
    a. After school programs for boys
    b. How much the sisters loved dance
    c. Friends having fun together
    d. How much the dad loves the twins

Animals of Yellowstone

Jason and his family are visiting Yellowstone National Park in Wyoming. Jason and his sister, Jennifer, are hoping to see some of the more special mammals that live in the park. Jason and Jennifer love photography and want to take pictures of the animals. The week before their trip, Jason had prepared a chart so they could figure out the best places to look for each animal and how likely they were to see them.

Animal	Habitat	Likely Location in the Park	Population
Grizzly Bear	forests, meadows	Lamar Valley, Mt. Washburn, Hayden Valley, Mammoth Hot Springs	500 - 650
Black Bear	forests, meadows	Lamar Valley, Mt. Washburn, Hayden Valley, Mammoth Hot Springs	280 - 610
Gray Wolf	forests, meadows	Lamar Valley, Mt. Washburn, Hayden Valley, Mammoth Hot Springs	less than 100
Elk	forests, meadows	Lamar Valley, Mt. Washburn, Hayden Valley, Mammoth Hot Springs, Old Faithful	15,000 – 25,000
Moose	river banks, forests	South Entrance, West Thumb	less than 500
Bison	meadows, grasslands	Lamar Valley, Mt. Washburn, Hayden Valley, Mammoth Hot Springs, Old Faithful	less than 3,500
Big Horn Sheep	cliffs, mountain slopes	Mt. Washburn, Mammoth Hot Springs	250 - 275

1. Why did Jason research the Yellowstone Animals?
   a. He wanted to know which animals lived in the park.
   b. He wanted to impress his sister.
   c. He wanted to find out how many animals there were.
   d. He wanted to know where to look for the animals.

2. Where are Jason and Jennifer most likely to see moose?
   a. South Entrance and West Thumb
   b. Lamar Valley and Mt. Washburn
   c. Mammoth Hot Springs and Hayden Valley
   d. South Entrance and Old Faithful

3. Which animal has the largest population?
   a. Moose
   b. Elk
   c. Gray Wolf
   d. Grizzly Bear

4. Information in this passage suggests
   a. Big Horn sheep live in more areas than any other animal.
   b. There are more grey wolves than moose.
   c. More animals live in forests and meadows.
   d. There are more predators than prey in the park.

5. From the context of this passage, what does the word "habitat" mean?
   a. A regular or usual action
   b. An unfamiliar area
   c. A place where animals store food for the winter
   d. An animal's home area

6. What evidence does the author give suggesting they will NOT see any grey wolves?
   a. The wolves live in forests and meadows.
   b. The wolves have the smallest population.
   c. The wolves live in meadows and grasslands.
   d. The wolves can be seen in Lamar Valley.

A Day in the City

Robby and his dad planned to spend Saturday in Washington, D.C. They had several stops planned, including Pentagon City, Arlington National Cemetery, and the Smithsonian. Because it costs so much to park in the city, Robby and his father take the subway the first Saturday of every month when they have a "boy's day" together.

"We have to look at a subway system map and make a chart so we can figure out which one is the best to use," said Robby's dad. "There are five different subway lines in the city: red, blue, orange, green, and yellow."

	Red Line	Blue Line	Orange Line	Green Line	Yellow Line
Pentagon City		x			x
The White House		x	X		
Smithsonian		x	X		
National Zoo	x				
National Archives				x	x
Arlington Cemetery		x			
National Air and Space Museum		x	X	x	x
International Spy Museum	x			x	x
Washington National Cathedral	x				

1. How will Robby and his dad get to all the places on their list?
   a. Walk
   b. Bus
   c. Car
   d. Subway

2. Robby and his dad can use the subway chart to help answer which of the following questions?
   a. What time does the subway arrive at the White House?
   b. How much does it cost to take the subway?
   c. Which subway lines would you take to get to the National Archives?
   d. How long will it take to get to Pentagon City?

3. Which of these best describes Robby and his father?
   a. They don't like to drive in the city.
   b. They enjoy doing things together.
   c. They think the subway schedule is too complicated.
   d. They think the subway is dirty and crowded.

4. Which of the following places could Robby and his dad visit while staying on **the same** subway line?
   a. The National Zoo and the Pentagon City
   b. The National Archives and the Washington National Cathedral
   c. The White House and the National Air and Space Museum
   d. Washington National Cathedral and Arlington Cemetery

5. Read the following dictionary entry for the word "chart."

Chart (*chahrt*) n. 1. a sheet arranging information into columns or tabs; 2. a map, especially a marine map; 3. a graphic representation; 4. an outline map showing special conditions or facts, such as a weather chart.

Which definition represents the meaning of "chart" as used in the passage?
   a. Definition 1
   b. Definition 2
   c. Definition 3
   d. Definition 4

6. What evidence does the author use to suggest that the Washington National Cathedral is a difficult location to reach?
   a. It is only on one subway line.
   b. The blue line has many more attractions.
   c. Robby and his dad are not planning to go there.
   d. It is near the International Spy Museum.

Family Names

Surnames are names that families share. They are passed down from generation to generation today, but this was not always the case.

Last names were first used in Europe during the middle Ages. People only had first names, so if three men named John lived in your village, it could get very confusing! However, if one John was a baker, one was an archer, and one was a barrel maker, you could tell them apart by calling them by their profession. John the baker became John Baker, John the archer became John Archer, and John the barrel maker became John Cooper.

Does your family name come from a job your ancestors had long ago?

Last Name	Occupation	Origin
Bender	Bow Maker	This name comes from the Old English word "bendbow," for someone who makes bows for archery.
Cartwright	Cart Maker/Repairer	People named Cartwright were early transportation engineers.
Fletcher	Arrow Maker/Seller	Fletcher comes from the French word "fleche," which means arrow.
Mason	Stone Worker	Masons built brick and stone buildings such as castles.
Parker	Gamekeeper	Parkers took care of the woodlands and wildlife, much like a park ranger today.
Saddler	Saddle Maker	This person made saddles for horses.
Steward	Manager	The word "steward" comes from Middle English and was the title of the person who managed someone else's estate or home.

1. What is the main idea of this chart?
   a. To explain family names based on a person's father
   b. To explain European family names from the Dark Ages
   c. To explain family names based on occupations
   d. To explain family names based on different languages

2. From the passage, the word "transportation" most likely means
   a. To move people or things
   b. To build ships
   c. To build wheels
   d. To ship items to another place

3. What evidence does the chart give to support the idea that last names come from occupations?

    a. Lists of famous people with those last names

    b. Lists the first person ever to use the name and their occupation

    c. Definitions of colors and their meanings

    d. Definitions and origins of occupational words

4. According to this passage, if your last name is Cook, your ancestor most likely

    a. Was a pig keeper.

    b. Was a chef.

    c. Was a candle maker.

    d. Was a beer maker.

5. Two of the last names are from related occupations. Which two?

    a. Fletcher and Bender

    b. Cartwright and Mason

    c. Parker and Steward

    d. Steward and Cartwright

6. From the passage, "surname" most likely means

    a. Manager

    b. Middle Ages

    c. Last name

    d. Occupation

Meteor Watching

Every year in August, the Perseid Meteor shower is visible to the naked eye and is a favorite for professional and amateur astronomers, alike.

Many people like the Perseid Meteor shower because it happens in the summer when people are on vacation, the nighttime temperatures are moderate, and the weather generally is good. People have been enjoying this summer sky show for over 2,000 years.

Meteors are little bits of rock and ice left over from a comet passing by. The Perseid meteors are from the comet Swift-Tuttle, which passes by Earth every 135 years. The comet leaves a debris trail through which the Earth passes every year on its way around the Sun.

As the Earth moves through the debris trail, the meteors hit the atmosphere and burn, leaving streaks of light across the sky. The best time to see this light show is in the very early morning when the moon is setting. You need to be away from city lights, with a dark, open sky to see the shooting stars at their best.

1. Which of the following choices gives the main idea of the passage?
    a. The meteor shower is boring.
    b. Watching meteor showers in the country is easy.
    c. The Perseid meteor shower is a favorite.
    d. Watching meteor showers in the city is hard.

2. What evidence does the author give to suggest that the Perseid shower only happens once a year?

    a. It only happens in August.
    b. The comet only passes by every 135 years.
    c. People have been watching the shower for 2000 years.
    d. The weather is good for the shower.

3. From the passage, what does the word "debris" most likely mean?

    a. A collection of things
    b. A comet's tail
    c. Scattered fragments of rock
    d. The orbit around the Sun.

4. Both the Earth and the Swift-Tuttle comet orbit the sun. What is the major difference between their orbits?

    a. The Earth is a planet with an atmosphere.
    b. The comet has two names.
    c. The comet has a debris trail.
    d. The Earth takes one year to orbit the sun, and the comet takes 135 years to orbit the sun.

5. What is the best summary of paragraph 2?

    a. People have enjoyed watching the shower for 2000 years.
    b. People enjoy watching the shower because it happens in the summer.
    c. People enjoy moderate temperatures.
    d. People enjoy being on vacation.

6. From the passage, what does the word "moderate" most likely mean?

    a. Extreme
    b. Average
    c. Mild
    d. Nonexistent

Written Expression

Do you know how to express yourself well in written form? It may seem as if learning how to express your thoughts in well-structured sentences and paragraphs which use proper vocabulary and follow the rules of grammar is no longer necessary. After all, in today's world, it seems as if most people only communicate through instant messages and texting. That may be true when you're communicating with your friends and family, but it's not true in general. To be successful in life, it's just as necessary now to be able to express yourself clearly as it ever was. These exercises will help you improve in this area.

Practice Test

Prepositions

Prepositions show the relationship of a noun or pronoun to another word or phrase. They show direction, position, or other relationships.

For the following sentences, underline the preposition in each one.
1. Nick ran between Nate and Evan.
2. Nate leaped over Evan playing leapfrog.
3. Evan climbed across the monkey bars.
4. Nate ran toward the slides.
5. Evan and Nick rode their bikes around the block.

Conjunctions

Conjunctions are connecting words that connect different parts of a sentence. There are three kinds of conjunctions. **Coordinating conjunctions** help to connect two equal parts of a sentence; **subordinating conjunctions** connect a dependent clause to a main clause; and **correlative conjunctions** are *pairs of words* that link balanced words or phrases.

Examples:
Coordinating: Nick *and* Evan went to the playground.
Subordinating: Nate can't go swimming *until* they come back.
Correlative: *Both* Evan *and* Nick wanted to ride dirt bikes.

For the following sentences, underline the conjunction and then write whether the conjunction is coordinating, subordinating, or correlative.

1. Nick and Nate rode their dirt bikes through the woods.
2. Evan waited to ride because there were only two bikes.
3. Neither Nate nor Evan can drive a car yet.
4. Nate rode over the ramp, although it was too high for Evan.
5. Nick wants to eat not only pizza, but also hamburgers.
6. Evan wants to go to the movies, but Nick wants to go swimming.
7. Nate would like to have hamburgers and pizza for lunch.
8. Either Evan or Nick can ride the larger dirt bike.
9. The boys will go swimming unless it's too cold.
10. Both Nate and Evan are in 5th grade.

Verb Tenses

Verbs are words that show action. For example, in the sentence "Nate ate his hamburger," "ate" is the verb because it shows what Nate did.
The tense of a verb tells you when the action takes place.
- The verb is in the present tense if the action is happening now.
- The verb is in the past tense if the action already has happened.
- The verb is in the future tense if the action is going to happen.

Examples:
Present: Nate licks his ice cream cone.
Past: Evan ate his hamburger.
Future: Nick will drink his soda after lunch.

For the sentences below, decide if the action is happening in the present, happened in the past, or will happen in the future. Underline the verb and choose the correct tense.

1. Nate and Evan will go to Vietnam this spring.
    a. Present
    b. Past
    c. Future

2. Their grandmother cooks pho noodles for the boys.
    a. Present
    b. Past
    c. Future

3. Last year, it rained every day they were in Vietnam.
   a. Present
   b. Past
   c. Future

4. The boys will visit Tran Quoc Pagoda this year.
   a. Present
   b. Past
   c. Future

5. Their grandmother lives outside of Hanoi, the capital city of Vietnam.
   a. Present
   b. Past
   c. Future

For the following sentences, write the verb in its correct tense in the blank.

6. The boys _____ (ride) the train last year.

7. Nick _____ (enjoy) watching the scenery from the train windows.

8. Evan _____ (read) a book if they take the train again.

9. Nate _____ (want) to fly last year.

10. All three boys _____ (play) checkers if they ride the train.

Write two sentences of your own about music. Use a series in one sentence and a date in the other.

11. _____

_____

_____

_____

_____

12. _____

_____

_____

_____

_____

Changing Sentences

To keep your reader interested, you need to have a variety of sentences. Some of them should be long, some short, some simple, and some complex.

Rules for changing sentences:
- You can combine two short sentences by moving key words and phrases from one sentence to another. (The aquarium is full of small fish. It is in my bedroom. Combined: The aquarium in my bedroom is full of small fish.)
- You can combine sentence with related ideas to make compound or complex sentences. To do this, you use conjunctions such as and, or, and because. (I am happy. I see a puppy. Combined: I am happy because I see a puppy.)

For the sentence pairs below, combine them to make more interesting sentences.

1. Nate and Evan go to the Houston Zoo. They go on Sundays.

_____

_____

2. Dragonflies live by the river. I am hoping to see some today.

_____

_____

3. Evan likes the monkeys. The monkeys live in the primate habitat.

_____

_____

4. Baboons are from African and Asia. They mostly live in zoos now.

_____

_____

5. Nick watches the baby giraffe. It tries to eat leaves from a tall tree.

_____

_____

Multiple Meaning Words

Some words have more than one meaning. There are two types of multiple meaning words: those that sound alike, or those that sound different.
- Words that sound alike
  - Homophones sound alike but are spelled differently. (*I **so** want to **sew** that button for you.*)
- Words that sound different
  - Heteronyms are spelled the same but sound different. (*It's hard to drive a **windy** road on a **windy** day.*)

Homophones

For the questions below, circle the correct homophone to match the meaning.
1. 9 minus 7   too   two
2. correct   write   right
3. not here but   there   they're
4. less than two   one   won
5. tossed   through   threw
6. make a mistake   air   err
7. walkway   isle   aisle
8. chewed and swallowed   ate   eight
9. deep or low   bass   base
10. uncovered   bare   bear

Heteronyms

Read the sentences below and circle the correct heteronym to fit the meaning in parenthesis.

1. The Polish furniture needs polish. (a substance to give a shiny surface)
2. I object to that object. (disapprove)
3. She was close enough to the window to close it. (to shut)
4. The bass drum had a bass painted on it. (a fish)
5. Mr. Jones is ready to present the present to the President. (to give formally)
6. Don't desert us just because we are in the desert. (to leave)
7. The dove dove for the food. (a bird)
8. Give me a minute and I'll show you minute particles in my microscope. (tiny)
9. The singer is here to record a new record. (to preserve in sound)
10. I refuse to take out the refuse. (to say no)

Greek and Latin roots and affixes

Knowing what the root word means, or understanding the affix, can help you to figure out the meaning of a new word.

For the sentences below, the Greek / Latin root or affix and its meaning have been provided. The sentences use a variation of this root word. Use the meaning of the Greek / Latin word to help you place the correct modern word in the right sentence.

1. Photo = light

    photograph   telephoto   photosynthesis   photogenic

    a. She certainly is _____4_____.
    b. My new camera takes a great _____1_____.
    c. This big lens helps take _____2_____ shots.
    d. Plants use _____3_____ to make food.

2. Aero = air

    aerobics   aerodynamics   aeronautics   aerate

    a. The study of wind flow over an object is called _____2_____.
    b. My mom takes a(n) _____1_____ exercise class.
    c. Poke holes in the soil to _____4_____ the roots of the plant.
    d. Scientists use _____3_____ to improve plane and space flight.

3. Dem = people

    democracy   demography   endemic   epidemic

    a. When a lot of people catch the same disease, it's known as a(n)
    _____4_____.

    b. America's form of government is a(n) _____1_____.
    c. The study of vital statistics such as birth rates is called
    _____2_____.
    d. A(n) _____3_____ disease is found in a particular place or people.

Context Clues

Learning how to guess words you don't know is an important skill, and one of the best ways to do that is with context clues. Use the rest of the sentence, or even the whole paragraph to figure out what an unfamiliar word might mean.

For the questions below, read the sentence and use context clues to choose the most likely meaning for the underlined word.

1. Robert's pet snake <u>slithered</u> across the floor.
    a. moved
    b. stopped
    c. hunted
    d. chased

2. We should <u>abolish</u> the "no hats" rule in class.
    a. start
    b. get rid of
    c. comply with
    d. agree with

3. I feel <u>deprived</u> when I can't play my guitar.
    a. damaged
    b. challenged
    c. happy
    d. denied

4. Wind Cave is <u>immense</u>! I can't see the top!
    a. huge
    b. small
    c. damp
    d. dark

5. The spy was very <u>nonchalant</u> as he walked slowly through the White House.
    a. happy
    b. sad
    c. calm
    d. excited

Reference Materials

Sometimes, to find the meaning of a word or learn how to pronounce it, you have to use reference materials. Reference materials can include dictionaries, encyclopedias, glossaries, or thesauruses.

For the questions below, a dictionary entry has been provided for you. Read it carefully and then answer the questions.

(1) **Miniature** (2) [ˈmin(ē)əCHər] (3) **adj.** of a much smaller size than normal
        noun. a thing that is much smaller than normal
        verb. represent on a smaller scale
(4) synonyms: diminutive, tiny, small

1. Which part of the entry tells you how to pronounce the word?
    a. 1
    b. 2
    c. 3
    d. 4

2. Which part of the entry tells you the definition(s) of the word?
    a. 1
    b. 2
    c. 3
    d. 4

3. Which part of the entry gives you words that have similar meanings?
    a. 1
    b. 2
    c. 3
    d. 4

4. Which part of the entry shows you how to spell the word correctly?
    a. 1
    b. 2
    c. 3
    d. 4

For the following questions, indicate which type of reference you would use to find the requested information.

a. Dictionary   b. Glossary   c. Thesaurus   d. Encyclopedia

5. Where could you find out more information about Los Dios de Muertos?

6. Where could you find out the definition of the word *narrator*?

7. Where could you find words with similar meanings to the word *protagonist*?

8. Where would you look to find out the meaning of an underlined word in your science book?

Figurative Language

Authors use figurative language such as similes, metaphors, alliteration, idioms, and onomatopoeia to help the reader paint a picture in their minds.

Simile – compares two ideas, feelings, or things using "like" or "as"
    Ex: Float like a butterfly
Metaphor – compares two ideas, feelings, or things without "like" or "as"
    Ex: The night sky is black velvet.
Alliteration – repetition of beginning sounds
    Ex: Al ate apples all around Albany.
Onomatopoeia – words that represent a sound
    Ex: Boom!
Idiom – a natural form of expression
    Ex: Out of the blue

Read the following sentences and choose the correct form of figurative language.

1. I've been working like a dog.
    a. simile
    b. metaphor
    c. alliteration
    d. onomatopoeia
    e. idiom

2. The dog barked and howled all night.
    a. simile
    b. metaphor
    c. alliteration
    d. onomatopoeia
    e. idiom

3. Red scarves are a dime a dozen.
    a. simile
    b. metaphor
    c. alliteration
    d. onomatopoeia
    e. idiom

4. Geoffrey has the heart of a lion.
    a. simile
    b. metaphor
    c. alliteration
    d. onomatopoeia
    e. idiom

5. Suzie sells seashells by the sea shore.
    a. simile
    b. metaphor
    c. alliteration
    d. onomatopoeia
    e. idiom

Synonyms and Antonyms

Another way authors keep their readers' interest is by using synonyms and antonyms. This keeps them from using the same words over and over.

Synonyms are words with nearly the same meaning as another word. (reply/answer)
Antonyms are words with opposite meanings. (wrong/right)

*For each of the sentences below, write a **synonym** for the underlined word.*

1. The <u>large</u> dog jumped on the fence.   _____
2. Math is very <u>difficult.</u>   _____
3. Jack and Jill went up the hill with a <u>pail</u>.   _____
4. Nate's dad was very <u>angry</u> with the boys.   _____
5. "Don't <u>speak</u> to me," said Julia.   _____

*For each of the sentences below, write an **antonym** for the underlined word.*

6. I love living in the <u>country</u>.   _____
7. The cookie jar is always <u>empty</u>.   _____
8. That dog is <u>ugly</u>!   _____
9. You have to <u>freeze</u> popsicles before you eat them.   _____

10. <u>Throw</u> me the ball!   _____

Mathematics

These exercises and problems will help you in your math classes. You'll solve problems involving addition, subtraction, division, multiplication, decimals, geometry, shapes, and graphs. You'll find a lot of helpful instructions along the way. Take your time and do your best, and then take the test at the end to see how you're doing.

Math Practice

Use what you learned about place value to sort and solve the problems below.

1. $3 + 400 + 4,000 + 20,000 + 50 =$ __24,453__
2. $50,000 + 700 + 10 + 5,000 + 8 =$ _____

3. $500 + 50 + 10,000 + 9,000 + 4 =$ 19,554
4. $8,000 + 100 + 30 + 2 + 20,000 =$ _____

5. $10,000 + 900 + 60 + 2,000 + 6 =$ _____
6. $90,000 + 300 + 50 + 9 + 3,000 =$ _____

7. $1 + 500 + 6,000 + 90,000 + 90 =$ _____
8. $700 + 70 + 50,000 + 6,000 + 2 =$ _____

9. $3,000 + 200 + 90 + 7 + 80,000 =$ _____
10. $5 + 900 + 7,000 + 20,000 + 10 =$ 27,915

11. $5,000 + 200 + 10 + 2 + 30,000 =$ _____
12. $600 + 80 + 60,000 + 2,000 + 9 =$ _____

13. $40,000 + 200 + 10 + 9,000 + 2 =$ _____
14. $9,000 + 300 + 50 + 9 + 70,000 =$ _____

15. $6 + 700 + 3,000 + 90,000 + 50 =$ _____
16. $8 + 300 + 1,000 + 40,000 + 20 =$ _____

17. $3,000 + 7 + 50 + 900 + 40,000 =$ _____
18. $100 + 60 + 10,000 + 4,000 + 1 =$ _____

19. $500 + 60 + 90,000 + 3,000 + 4 =$ _____
20. $7 + 800 + 9,000 + 30,000 + 10 =$ 39,817

Round the following numbers to the nearest thousand.

1. 2,563 ____3,000____
2. 9,198 _____
3. 1,423 _4,000_
4. 7,712 _____
5. 3,300 _____

6. 4,219 _____
7. 5,756 _____
8. 8,154 _____
9. 6,069 _6,000_
10. 1,995 _____

Round the following numbers to the nearest ten-thousand.

11. 39,092 _40,000_
12. 19,917 _____
13. 93,254 _____
14. 56,055 _____
15. 70,856 _____

16. 77,150 _____
17. 33,809 _____
18. 35,451 _40,000_
19. 20,901 _20,000_
20. 48,599 _____

Round the following numbers to the nearest hundred-thousand.

21. 274,333 _____
22. 596,559 _____
23. 221,324 _200,000_
24. 530,708 _____
25. 189,365 _____

26. 317,110 _300,000_
27. 882,658 _____
28. 610,567 _____
29. 789,381 _____
30. 109,277 _100,000_

To estimate a sum or difference, round each number.
Then add or subtract the rounded numbers.

Estimate and solve the problems below.

1. 6,281 →
    +3,552 →

2. 4,782 →
    +1,321 →

3. 9,423 →
    +6,599 →

4. 5,192 →
    +4,807 →

5. 2,991 →
    +5,841 →

6. 7,510 →
    +7,291 →

7. 1,690 →
    +4,501 →

8. 3,908 →
    +4,687 →

9. 9,499 →
    + 532 →

10. 3,641 →
     -2,487 →

11. 8,961 →
     -4,540 →

12. 7,299 →
     -5,607 →

13. 4,701 →
     -3,112 →

14. 9,475 →
     -7,500 →

15. 3,559 →
     -1,890 →

16. 4,115 →
     - 805 →

17. 5,602 →
     -2,199 →

18. 7,999 →
     -5,999 →

Solve the problems below using regrouping.

1. 3,541,277
    6,129,245
    + 2,382,107
    —————————

2. 2,711,015
    3,844,362
    + 1,332,745
    —————————

3. 5,008,694
    3,992,406
    + 8,264,367
    —————————

4. 8,267,200
    7,164,245
    + 6,277,594
    —————————

5. 5,466,999
    3,050,638
    + 6,105,347
    —————————

6. 7,548,007
    2,215,635
    + 1,365,815
    —————————

7. 9,147,129
    6,308,905
    + 4,315,707
    —————————

8. 5,113,799
    5,564,002
    + 6,465,355
    —————————

9. 1,648,912
    3,154,099
    + 5,367,474
    —————————

10. 6,905,011
    4,322,966
    + 3,375,378
    —————————

11. 6,475,619
    9,504,242
    + 7,289,071
    —————————

12. 1,299,151
    3,637,889
    + 8,652,234
    —————————

13. 3,552,910
    7,313,577
    + 4,429,964
    —————————

14. 6,008,799
    5,027,346
    + 6,244,310
    —————————

15. 1,224,799
    1,496,843
    + 9,841,000
    —————————

16. 4,208,577
    5,995,685
    + 5,372,129
    —————————

17. 6,141,654
    1,764,889
    + 7,633,924
    —————————

18. 5,639,047
    6,129,885
    + 3,445,369
    —————————

19. 9,665,007
    8,682,420
    + 4,341,204
    —————————

20. 5,245,895
    6,636,635
    + 8,547,118
    —————————

Use what you learned about borrowing to solve the problems below.

1. 32,445,311
    − 19,306,805

2. 54,009,812
    − 23,329,605

3. 72,511,420
    − 49,964,122

4. 43,652,019
    − 7,994,364

5. 17,457,333
    − 9,864,127

6. 85,674,152
    − 39,200,997

7. 55,925,321
    −   365,544

8. 90,899,425
    − 1,621,678
    89,277,747

9. 69,129,364
    − 34,330,657

10. 84,994,657
     − 65,732,566

11. 88,299,882
     − 2,164,295

12. 39,599,635
     − 10,124,988

13. 67,290,975
     − 2,364,963
     64,926,012

14. 50,400,991
     − 6,536,027
     43,864,964

15. 42,633,635
     − 12,396,864

16. 95,155,964
     − 57,377,337

17. 82,112,650
     −   820,941

18. 75,644,340
     − 38,637,652

19. 59,965,122
     − 3,637,569

20. 93,050,002
     − 54,864,632

21. 66,965,362
     −   167,064

22. 92,338,674
     − 17,211,995

23. 44,294,632
     − 29,009,367

24. 84,962,366
     − 52,507,999

To multiply a four-digit number by a three-digit number, start in the ones place and then use basic multiplication and addition rules. Don't forget to use what you've learned about regrouping.

Solve the problems below.

1. 6,584
   x 324

2. 3,291
   x 105

3. 8,347
   x 137

4. 4,551
   x 244

5. 9,067
   x 320

6. 6,561
   x 439

7. 7,812
   x 140

8. 3,302
   x 259

9. 5,191
   x 341

10. 4,073
    x 326

11. 8,651
    x 560

12. 3,291
    x 424

13. 5,067
    x 682

14. 5,297
    x 119

15. 9,436
    x 207

16. 3,624
    x 329

17. 7,117
    x 708

18. 5,930
    x 132

19. 8,175
    x 985

20. 6,408
    x 560

Write out the exponents below and solve. Use the boxes to work out the problems,

1. $8^2 =$ _____ = _____

2. $6^5 =$ _____ = _____

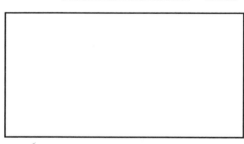

3. $7^4 =$ _____ = _____

4. $3^8 =$ _____ = _____

5. $4^3 =$ _____ = _____

6. $5^5 =$ _____ = _____

Solve these problems. Some may not have remainders.

1.

$$3,229\,r8$$
$$12\overline{)38,756}$$
$$\underline{-36}$$
$$27$$
$$\underline{-24}$$
$$35$$
$$\underline{-24}$$
$$116$$
$$\underline{-108}$$
$$8$$

2. $34\overline{)85,097}$

3. $57\overline{)96,134}$

4. $29\overline{)64,893}$

5. $45\overline{)95,507}$

6. $61\overline{)35,692}$

7. $32\overline{)96,599}$

8. $43\overline{)77,039}$

9. $59\overline{)32,072}$

10. $86\overline{)90,965}$

11. $71\overline{)80,099}$

$$1128\,r11$$
$$71$$
$$90$$
$$71$$
$$199$$
$$142$$
$$579$$
$$568$$
$$11$$

12. $27\overline{)43,992}$

To add fractions with different denominators, first find a common denominator. Then add the numerators.

Solve each problem. Find each common denominator and sum.

1.

$$\frac{12}{18} = \frac{12}{18}$$

$$-\frac{2}{9} = \frac{4}{18}$$

$$\frac{8}{18}$$

2.

$$\frac{4}{7} = \underline{\quad}$$

$$-\frac{3}{21} = \underline{\quad}$$

$$\underline{\quad}$$

3.

$$\frac{7}{9} = \frac{35}{45}$$

$$-\frac{20}{45} = \frac{20}{45}$$

$$\frac{15}{45} = \frac{1}{3}$$

4.

$$\frac{28}{35} = \underline{\quad}$$

$$-\frac{3}{5} = \underline{\quad}$$

$$\underline{\quad}$$

5.

$$\frac{3}{7} = \underline{\quad}$$

$$-\frac{18}{63} = \underline{\quad}$$

$$\underline{\quad}$$

6.

$$\frac{36}{42} = \underline{\quad}$$

$$-\frac{5}{7} = \underline{\quad}$$

$$\underline{\quad}$$

7.

$$\frac{81}{81} = \underline{\quad}$$

$$-\frac{6}{9} = \underline{\quad}$$

$$\underline{\quad}$$

8.

$$\frac{8}{9} = \underline{\quad}$$

$$-\frac{12}{36} = \underline{\quad}$$

$$\underline{\quad}$$

9.

$$\frac{6}{7} = \underline{\quad}$$

$$-\frac{21}{49} = \underline{\quad}$$

$$\underline{\quad}$$

10.

$$\frac{8}{9} = \underline{\quad}$$

$$-\frac{12}{54} = \underline{\quad}$$

$$\underline{\quad}$$

11.

$$\frac{5}{6} = \frac{40}{48}$$

$$-\frac{16}{48} = \frac{16}{48}$$

$$\frac{24}{48} = \frac{1}{2}$$

12.

$$\frac{32}{36} = \underline{\quad}$$

$$-\frac{5}{9} = \underline{\quad}$$

$$\underline{\quad}$$

To change a fraction to an equivalent fraction, multiply the numerator and the denominator by the same number.

Fill in the blanks to find equivalent fractions, then subtract.

1. $\dfrac{2}{4} = \dfrac{10}{20}$

    $-\dfrac{6}{20} = -\dfrac{6}{20}$

    $\dfrac{4}{20}$

2. $\dfrac{14}{15} = \dfrac{}{15}$

    $-\dfrac{4}{5} = -\dfrac{}{15}$

    $\dfrac{}{}$

3. $\dfrac{13}{18} = \dfrac{}{18}$

    $-\dfrac{2}{6} = -\dfrac{}{18}$

    $\dfrac{}{}$

4. $\dfrac{35}{40} = \dfrac{}{40}$

    $-\dfrac{2}{4} = -\dfrac{}{40}$

    $\dfrac{}{}$

5. $\dfrac{5}{6} = \dfrac{}{48}$

    $-\dfrac{29}{48} = -\dfrac{}{48}$

    $\dfrac{}{}$

6. $\dfrac{16}{24} = \dfrac{}{24}$

    $-\dfrac{5}{8} = -\dfrac{}{24}$

    $\dfrac{}{}$

7. $\dfrac{36}{49} = \dfrac{}{49}$

    $-\dfrac{3}{7} = -\dfrac{}{49}$

    $\dfrac{}{}$

8. $\dfrac{5}{6} = \dfrac{40}{54}$

    $-\dfrac{29}{54} = -\dfrac{29}{54}$

    $\dfrac{4}{54}$

9. $\dfrac{63}{81} = \dfrac{}{81}$

    $+\dfrac{6}{9} = -\dfrac{}{81}$

    $\dfrac{}{}$

10. $\dfrac{54}{63} = \dfrac{}{63}$

    $-\dfrac{5}{9} = -\dfrac{}{63}$

    $\dfrac{}{}$

11. $\dfrac{27}{48} = \dfrac{27}{48}$

    $-\dfrac{4}{8} = -\dfrac{24}{48}$

    $\dfrac{3}{48} = \dfrac{1}{16}$

12. $\dfrac{35}{50} = \dfrac{}{100}$

    $-\dfrac{50}{100} = -\dfrac{}{100}$

    $\dfrac{}{}$

To add, subtract, multiply or divide mixed numbers by other fractions, we need to convert the mixed number to an improper fraction.

Step 1:	Step 2:	Step 3:
Multiply the whole number by the denominator.	Add the numerator to the product.	Keep the denominator the same.
$2\frac{1}{4} = \frac{2 \times 4}{4}$	$2\frac{1}{4} = \frac{2 \times 4 + 1}{4} = \frac{9}{4}$	$2\frac{1}{4} = \frac{9}{4}$

Convert each mixed number to an improper fraction.

1. $3\frac{4}{3} = \frac{13}{3}$

2. $8\frac{6}{4} = $ —

3. $2\frac{9}{2} = $ —

4. $6\frac{2}{5} = $ —

5. $9\frac{5}{10} = $ —

6. $4\frac{1}{5} = $ —

7. $3\frac{4}{7} = $ —

8. $1\frac{11}{3} = $ —

9. $5\frac{1}{5} = $ —

10. $8\frac{6}{3} = $ —

11. $4\frac{7}{5} = $ —

12. $2\frac{2}{8} = $ —

13. $9\frac{7}{5} = $ —

14. $7\frac{6}{3} = $ —

15. $6\frac{3}{11} = $ —

16. $3\frac{7}{3} = $ —

17. $1\frac{15}{22} = $ —

18. $2\frac{6}{9} = $ —

19. $8\frac{2}{4} = $ —

20. $9\frac{5}{3} = $ —

Use what you learned about adding numbers with decimals to find the totals to the questions below. Show your work in the boxes.

1: 164.99 + 805.46 + .75

2: 150.92 + 321 + 50.24

3: 95.56 + 128.7 + 9.23

4: 389.04 + 84.99 + 6.15

5: 18.56 + 991.5 + 525.09

6: 61.91 + 571.17 + 223.09

7. 7.56 + 75.61 + 756.1

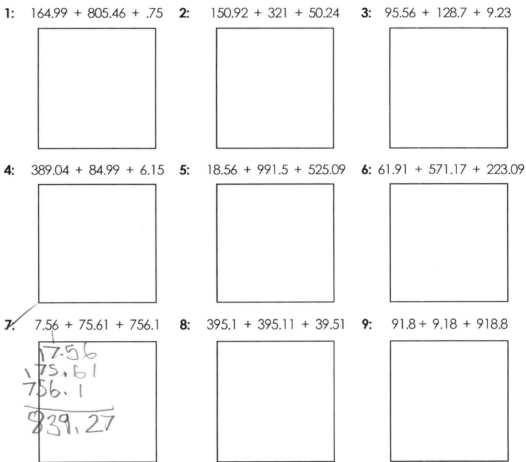

$$7.56$$
$$75.61$$
$$756.1$$
$$839.27$$

8: 395.1 + 395.11 + 39.51

9: 91.8 + 9.18 + 918.8

Find the totals below.

1.
```
  2,418.09
  4,334.49
    712.64
+ 1,482.11
```

2.
```
  6,967.24
     34.13
  5,110.37
+ 2,326.22
```

3.
```
  2,126.94
  3,615.03
     24.77
+ 4,331.62
```

4.
```
  7,269.81
  1,382.43
    409.30
+     3.99
```

5.
```
    604.88
  7,291.39
  3,036.13
+ 9,123.24
```

6.
```
  4,168.68
  5,055.33
  4,333.07
+   659.37
```

7.
```
  9,224.54
     75.31
      4.52
+ 3,012.10
```

8.
```
    482.00
  3,312.67
  4,999.60
+    20.54
```

9.
```
  6,287.90
    961.24
    823.36
+ 2,682.48
```

10.
```
    329.58
  3,677.41
  9,003.36
+    51.27
```

11.
```
  7,622.31
    301.02
    440.68
+ 2,539.88
```

12.
```
  5,880.99
  5,951.50
     47.66
+     9.72
```

13.
```
  4,408.12
  8,399.99
    254.17
  2,765.55
+ 7,321.01
```

14.
```
     88.78
  9,100.59
     65.34
  3,036.66
+     7.92
```

15.
```
  1,448.39
  6,691.15
  2,308.54
    279.02
+    35.37
```

16.
```
  5,651.14
  9,842.59
  2,000.77
  2,621.22
+ 2,903.00
```

Subtract the amounts below.

1. 49.9262
   − 32.6139

2. 69.8420
   − 29.9609

3. 39.7124
   − 18.2570

4. 84.4962
   − 38.8691

5. 720.581
   − 556.512

6. 521.003
   − 352.109

7. 120.589
   − 100.075

8. 264.892
   − 155.684

9. 49,078.2
   − 38,865.1

10. 8,009.01
   − 6,420.57

11. 9,569.25
   − 3,365.72

12. 7.65940
   − 2.29995

13. 3,965.21
   − 1,788.95

14. 548.722
   − 345.871

15. 2.99265
   − .95846

16. 90.0364
   − 77.8205
      12.2159

17. 89,756.1
   − 15,672.7

18. 77,582.1
   − 56,963.8
      20,618.3

19. 33,587.2
   − 19,985.7

20. 9,987.02
   − 8,908.25

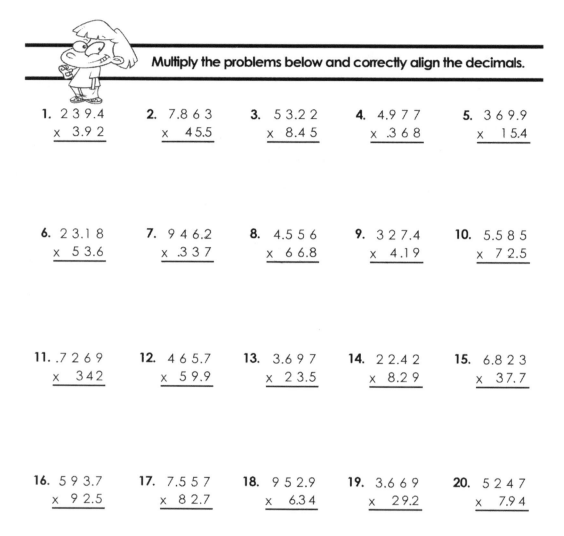

Multiply the problems below and correctly align the decimals.

1. 2 3 9.4
    x 3.9 2
    _____

2. 7.8 6 3
    x   4 5.5
    _____

3. 5 3.2 2
    x 8.4 5
    _____

4. 4.9 7 7
    x .3 6 8
    _____

5. 3 6 9.9
    x   1 5.4
    _____

6. 2 3.1 8
    x 5 3.6
    _____

7. 9 4 6.2
    x .3 3 7
    _____

8. 4.5 5 6
    x 6 6.8
    _____

9. 3 2 7.4
    x 4.1 9
    _____

10. 5.5 8 5
     x 7 2.5
     _____

11. .7 2 6 9
     x   3 4 2
     _____

12. 4 6 5.7
     x 5 9.9
     _____

13. 3.6 9 7
     x 2 3.5
     _____

14. 2 2.4 2
     x 8.2 9
     _____

15. 6.8 2 3
     x 3 7.7
     _____

16. 5 9 3.7
     x 9 2.5
     _____

17. 7.5 5 7
     x 8 2.7
     _____

18. 9 5 2.9
     x 6.3 4
     _____

19. 3.6 6 9
     x 2 9.2
     _____

20. 5 2 4 7
     x 7.9 4
     _____

- A **polygon** is a closed plane figure made up of 3 or more line segments.
- Polygons that have all sides of equal length are called regular polygons.
- Polygons are named depending on the number of lines that form their boundaries.

Here are some examples of **polygons**:

| **Triangle:** | **Quadrilateral** | **Pentagon** |
| A polygon with three sides | A polygon with four sides. | A polygon with five sides |

A **quadrilateral** is a four-sided polygon. Here are some types of **quadrilateral** shapes:

Rectangle: A parallelogram with four right angles.

Square: A parallelogram with four congruent sides and four right angles.

Trapezoid: A quadrilateral with only one pair of parallel sides.

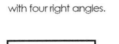

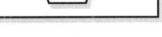

Parallelogram: A quadrilateral with two pairs of opposite sides parallel.

Rhombus: A parallelogram with four congruent sides.

To find the **area** of a **trapezoid** use this formula:

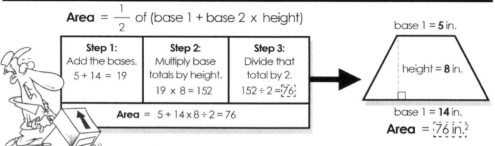

$$\text{Area} = \frac{1}{2} \text{ of (base 1 + base 2 x height)}$$

Step 1: Add the bases. 5 + 14 = 19	Step 2: Multiply base totals by height. 19 x 8 = 152	Step 3: Divide that total by 2. 152 ÷ 2 = 76

Area = 5 + 14 x 8 ÷ 2 = 76

base 1 = **5** in.

height = **8** in.

base 1 = **14** in.

Area = 76 in.²

Find the area of each trapezoid. Write the problem out.

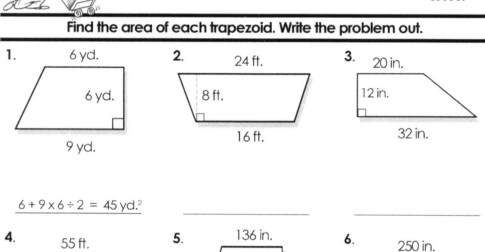

1.
6 yd.

6 yd.

9 yd.

2.
24 ft.

8 ft.

16 ft.

3.
20 in.

12 in.

32 in.

6 + 9 x 6 ÷ 2 = 45 yd.²

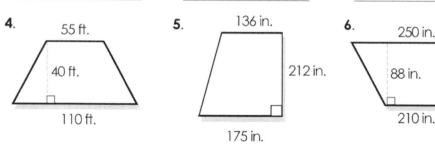

4.
55 ft.

40 ft.

110 ft.

5.
136 in.

212 in.

175 in.

6.
250 in.

88 in.

210 in.

_____

_____

_____

- Angles are determined by points and rays.
- This angle is named - ∠ABC.
- This angle is made up of rays AB and CB.
- The vertex of ∠ABC is the point B.

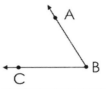

Identify the vertex, rays and names of each angle.

1.

Angle: ___ABC___

Vertex: ___B___

Rays: ___AB, CB___

2.

Angle: _____

Vertex: _____

Rays: _____

3.

Angle: _____

Vertex: _____

Rays: _____

4.

Angle: _____

Vertex: _____

Rays: _____

5.

Angle: _____

Vertex: _____

Rays: _____

6.

Angle: _____

Vertex: _____

Rays: _____

7.

Angle: _____

Vertex: _____

Rays: _____

8.

Angle: _____

Vertex: _____

Rays: _____

9.

Angle: _____

Vertex: _____

Rays: _____

10.

Angle: _____

Vertex: _____

Rays: _____

11.

Angle: _____

Vertex: _____

Rays: _____

12.

Angle: _____

Vertex: _____

Rays: _____

Now we will learn about the components that make up a circle.
With a circle we have the **radius**, **diameter** and the **circumference**.
Knowing these components will help you to solve problems related to circles.

Radius

The **radius** of a circle is the distance from the circle's center
point to any point on the circle. It can be used to determine
a circle's diameter, circumference and area. Because of
the circle's shape, the radius can be drawn in anywhere
in the center of the circle.

Use this formula to find the radius of a circle:
Radius = Diameter ÷ 2

Diameter

The **diameter** of a circle is the length of a straight line through
the center of a circle and touching two points on its edge,
the diameter is twice the measurement of the radius. It is
the longest distance across the circle. If the diameter of
a circle is known, dividing it by two will equal the radius.

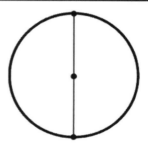

Use this formula to find the diameter of a circle:
Diameter = Radius x 2

Circumference

A circle's **circumference** is the distance around the circle.
To determine the circumference of a circle, multiply the
diameter by pi (π), or multiply the radius by 2 then multiply
by pi (π). π is a Greek letter used in math to represent 3.14.

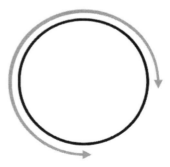

Use this formula to find the diameter of a circle:
Circumference = π x diameter or π x radius x 2

A circle's **circumference** is the distance around the circle. To determine the circumference of a circle, multiply the diameter by pi (π), or multiply the radius by 2 then multiply by pi (π). π is a Greek letter used in mathematics to represent 3.14.

Radius = 4 cm.   **Diameter** = 8 cm.

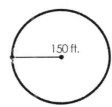

4 cm.   8 cm.

Circumference   **Circumference**
4 x 3.14 x 2 = 25.12   8 x 3.14 = 25.12

Use these formulas to find the circumference of a circle:
Circumference = (π x diameter) or (π x radius x 2)
Circumference = (3.14 x diameter) or (3.14 x radius x 2)

Using the radius and diameter, determine the circumference of each circle below.

1.

55 in.

2.
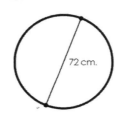
72 cm.

3.
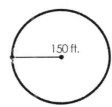
150 ft.

Circumference: _____**345.4 in.**_____   Circumference: _____   Circumference: _____

4.
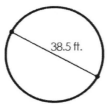
38.5 ft.

5.

531.4 in.

6.
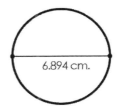
6.894 cm.

Circumference: _____   Circumference: _____   Circumference: _____

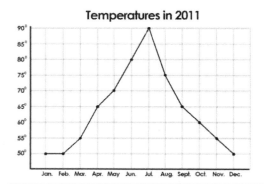

Temperatures in 2011

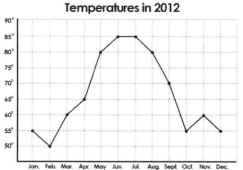

Temperatures in 2012

Use the graphs above to answer the questions below.

1. In which year was August hotter? _____

2. In which year was December colder? _____

3. What was the hottest temperature in 2012? _____

4. In 2011 what was the temperature in January? _____

5. In 2012 what was the temperature in January? _____

6. What was the coldest month in 2012? _____

7. What was the hottest month in 2011? _____

8. How much cooler was it in January 2011 than it was January in 2012? _____

9. What was the hottest temperature in 2011? _____

10. In 2011 what was the temperature in October? _____

11. In 2012 what was the temperature in October? _____

12. How much hotter was it in May 2012 than it was May in 2011? _____

13. Compared to April 2011, did the temperature rise, fall, or

    stay the same in April 2012? _____

14. Which year had the highest temperature? _____

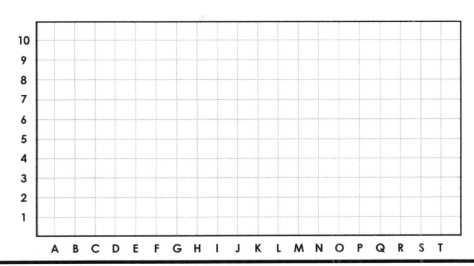

Using the coordinates below, plot the points on the graph above.
Draw a line between the points on the graph to create geometric shapes
and the write the name for each shape in the blanks.

1. A4, B1, E1, F4   trapezoid

2. G3, i3, G1, i1   _____

3. H6, L6, H4, L4   _____

4. P7, R10, T7   _____

5. F7, i10, L10, i7   _____

6. N8, M5, N2, O5   _____

7. P4, R5, T4, Q1, S1   _____

Answers

Whole Numbers

Place Value
1. 24,453
2. 55,718
3. 19,554
4. 28,132
5. 12,966
6. 93,359
7. 96,591
8. 56,772
9. 83,297
10. 27,915
11. 35,212
12. 62,689
13. 49,212
14. 79,359
15. 93,756
16. 41,328
17. 43,957
18. 14,161
19. 93,564
20. 39,817

Rounding
1. 3,000
2. 9,000
3. 1,000
4. 8,000
5. 3,000
6. 4,000
7. 6,000
8. 8,000
9. 6,000
10. 2,000
11. 40,000
12. 20,000
13. 90,000
14. 60,000
15. 70,000
16. 80,000

17. 30,000
18. 40,000
19. 20,000
20. 50,000
21. 300,000
22. 600,000
23. 200,000
24. 500,000
25. 200,000
26. 300,000
27. 900,000
28. 600,000
29. 800,000
30. 100,000

Addition with Rounding
1. 6,000 + 4,000 = 10,000
2. 5,000 + 1,000 = 6,000
3. 9,000 + 7,000 = 16,000
4. 5,000 + 5,000 = 10,000
5. 3,000 + 6,000 = 9,000
6. 8,000 + 7,000 = 15,000
7. 2,000 + 5,000 = 7,000
8. 4,000 + 5,000 = 9,000
9. 9,000 + 500 = 9,500
10. 4,000 - 2,000 = 2,000
11. 9,000 - 5,000 = 4,000
12. 7,000 - 6,000 = 1,000
13. 5,000 - 3,000 = 2,000
14. 9,000 - 8,000 = 1,000
15. 4,000 - 2,000 = 2,000
16. 4,000 - 800 = 3,200
17. 6,000 - 2,000 = 4,000
18. 8,000 - 6,000 = 2,000

Addition with Regrouping
1. 12,052,629
2. 7,888,122
3. 17,265,467
4. 21,709,039
5. 14,622,984
6. 11,129,457
7. 19,771,741

8. 17,143,156
9. 10,170,485
10. 14,603,355
11. 23,268,932
12. 13,589,274
13. 15,296,451
14. 17,280,455
15. 12,562,642
16. 15,576,391
17. 15,540,467
18. 15,214,301
19. 22,688,631
20. 20,429,648

Subtraction with Borrowing
1. 13,138,506
2. 30,680,207
3. 22,547,298
4. 35,657,655
5. 7,593,206
6. 46,473,155
7. 55,559,777
8. 89,277,747
9. 34,798,707
10. 19,262,091
11. 86,135,587
12. 29,474,647
13. 64,926,012
14. 43,864,964
15. 30,236,771
16. 37,778,627
17. 81,291,709
18. 37,006,688
19. 56,327,553
20. 38,185,370
21. 66,798,298
22. 75,126,679
23. 15,285,265
24. 32,454,367

Multi-Digit Multiplication
1. 2,133,216
2. 345,555
3. 1,143,539
4. 1,110,444
5. 2,901,440
6. 2,880,279
7. 1,093,680
8. 855,218
9. 1,770,131
10. 1,327,798
11. 4,844,560
12. 1,395,384
13. 3,455,694
14. 630,343
15. 1,953,252
16. 1,192,296
17. 5,038,836
18. 782,760
19. 8,052,375
20. 3,588,480

Exponents
1. 8 x 8 = 64
2. 6 x 6 x 6 x 6 x 6 = 7,776
3. 7 x 7 x 7 x 7 = 2,401
4. 3 x 3 x 3 x 3 x 3 x 3 x 3 x 3 = 6,561
5. 4 x 4 x 4 = 64
6. 5 x 5 x 5 x 5 x 5 = 3,125

Division
1. 3,229 r 8
2. 2,502 r 29
3. 1,686 r 32
4. 2,237 r 20
5. 2,122 r 17
6. 585 r 7
7. 3,018 r 23
8. 1,791 r 26
9. 543 r 35
10. 1,057 r 63
11. 1,128 r 11
12. 1,629 r 9

Common Denominators

1. $\dfrac{12}{18} - \dfrac{4}{18} = \dfrac{8}{18}$

2. $\dfrac{4}{7} - \dfrac{1}{7} = \dfrac{3}{7}$

3. $\dfrac{7}{9} - \dfrac{4}{9} = \dfrac{5}{9}$

4. $\dfrac{4}{5} - \dfrac{3}{5} = \dfrac{1}{5}$

5. $\dfrac{3}{7} - \dfrac{2}{7} = \dfrac{1}{7}$

6. $\dfrac{6}{7} - \dfrac{5}{7} = \dfrac{1}{7}$

7. $\dfrac{9}{9} - \dfrac{6}{9} = \dfrac{3}{9}$

8. $\dfrac{8}{9} - \dfrac{3}{9} = \dfrac{5}{9}$

9. $\dfrac{6}{7} - \dfrac{3}{7} = \dfrac{3}{7}$

10. $\dfrac{8}{9} - \dfrac{2}{9} = \dfrac{6}{9}$

11. $\dfrac{5}{6} - \dfrac{2}{6} = \dfrac{3}{6}$

12. $\dfrac{8}{9} - \dfrac{5}{9} = \dfrac{3}{9}$

Equivalent Fractions

1. $\dfrac{10}{20} - \dfrac{6}{20} = \dfrac{4}{20}$

2. $\dfrac{14}{15} - \dfrac{12}{15} = \dfrac{2}{15}$

3. $\dfrac{13}{18} - \dfrac{6}{18} = \dfrac{7}{18}$

4. $\dfrac{35}{40} - \dfrac{20}{40} = \dfrac{15}{40}$

5. $\dfrac{40}{48} - \dfrac{29}{48} = \dfrac{11}{48}$

6. $\dfrac{16}{24} - \dfrac{15}{24} = \dfrac{1}{24}$

7. $\dfrac{36}{49} - \dfrac{21}{49} = \dfrac{15}{49}$

8. $\dfrac{45}{54} = \dfrac{29}{54} = \dfrac{16}{54}$

9. $\dfrac{63}{81} - \dfrac{54}{81} = \dfrac{9}{81}$

10. $\dfrac{54}{63} - \dfrac{35}{63} = \dfrac{19}{63}$

11. $\dfrac{27}{48} - \dfrac{24}{48} = \dfrac{3}{48}$

12. $\dfrac{70}{100} - \dfrac{50}{100} = \dfrac{20}{100}$

Mixed Numbers and Improper Fractions

1. $\frac{13}{3}$
2. $\frac{38}{4}$
3. $\frac{13}{2}$
4. $\frac{32}{5}$
5. $\frac{95}{10}$
6. $\frac{21}{5}$
7. $\frac{25}{7}$
8. $\frac{14}{3}$
9. $\frac{26}{5}$
10. $\frac{30}{3}$
11. $\frac{27}{5}$
12. $\frac{18}{8}$
13. $\frac{52}{5}$
14. $\frac{27}{3}$
15. $\frac{69}{11}$
16. $\frac{16}{3}$
17. $\frac{37}{22}$
18. $\frac{24}{9}$
19. $\frac{34}{4}$
20. $\frac{32}{3}$

Adding Decimals 1

1. 971.2
2. 522.16
3. 233.49
4. 480.18
5. 1,535.15
6. 856.17
7. 839.27
8. 829.72
9. 1,019.78

Adding Decimals 2
1. 8,947.33
2. 14,437.96
3. 10,098.36
4. 9,065.53
5. 20,055.64
6. 14,216.45
7. 12,316.47
8. 8,814.81
9. 10,754.98
10. 13,061.62
11. 10,903.89
12. 11,889.87
13. 23,148.84
14. 12,299.29
15. 10,762.47
16. 23,018.72

Subtracting Decimals
1. 17.3123
2. 39.8811
3. 21.4554
4. 45.6271
5. 164.069
6. 168.894
7. 20.514
8. 109.208
9. 10,213.10
10. 1,588.44
11. 6,203.53
12. 5.35945
13. 2,176.26
14. 202.851
15. 2.03419
16. 12.2159
17. 74,083.40
18. 20,618.30
19. 13,601.50
20. 1,078.77

Multiplying Decimals
1. 938.448
2. 357.7665
3. 449.709
4. 1.831536
5. 5696.46
6. 1,242.448
7. 318.8694
8. 304.3408
9. 1,371.806
10. 404.9125
11. 248.5998
12. 27,895.43
13. 86.8795
14. 185.8618
15. 257.2271
16. 54,917.25
17. 624.9639
18. 6,041.386
19. 107.1348
20. 41,661.18

Finding Area of Trapezoid
1. $6 + 9 \times 6 \div 2 = 45$ yds.^{2}
2. $24 + 16 \times 8 \div 2 = 160$ ft.^{2}
3. $20 + 32 \times 12 \div 2 = 312$ in.^{2}
4. $55 + 110 \times 40 \div 2 = 3,300$ ft.^{2}
5. $136 + 175 \times 212 \div 2 = 32,966$ in.^{2}
6. $250 + 210 \times 88 \div 2 = 20,240$ in.^{2}

Angle, Vertex, Rays

1. Angle: ABC	Vertex: B	Rays: AB, CB
2. Angle: 123	Vertex: 2	Rays: 12, 23
3. Angle: QRS	Vertex: R	Rays: SR, QR
4. Angle: XYZ	Vertex: Y	Rays: XY, YZ
5. Angle: 456	Vertex: 5	Rays: 45, 56
6. Angle: EFG	Vertex: F	Rays: EF, EG
7. Angle: MNO	Vertex: N	Rays: MN, NO
8. Angle: 678	Vertex: 7	Rays: 67, 78
9. Angle: DEF	Vertex: E	Rays: FE, DE
10. Angle: 789	Vertex: 8	Rays: 78, 89
11. Angle: 012	Vertex: 1	Rays: 01, 12
12. Angle: UVW	Vertex: V	Rays: UV, VW

Finding Circumference
1. 345.4 in.
2. 226.08 cm.
3. 942 ft.
4. 120.89 ft.
5. 3,337.192 in.
6. 21.64716 cm.

Reading Graphs
1. 2012
2. 2011
3. 85 degrees
4. 50 degrees
5. 55 degrees
6. Feb
7. July
8. 5 degrees
9. 90 degrees
10. 60 degrees
11. 55 degrees
12. 10 degrees
13. Stayed the same
14. 2011

Coordinates and Graphs

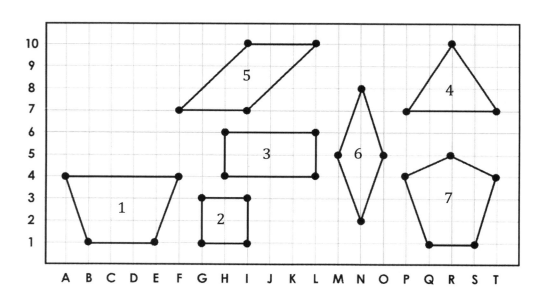

No.	Answer
1	trapezoid
2	square
3	rectangle
4	triangle
5	parallelogram
6	rhombus
7	pentagon

Practice Test

1. Simplify: $\{5 \times [9 - (4 \div 2) - 5]\} + 11 =$
   a. 21
   b. 27
   c. 49
   d. 71

2. Express the calculation "subtract 4 from 18, then divide by 7."
   a. $(4 - 18) \div 7$
   b. $4 - 18 \div 7$
   c. $(18 - 4) \div 7$
   d. $18 - 4 \div 7$

3. Choose two sequences so that the terms of one sequence are three times the corresponding terms of the other sequence.

   "add 2"   0, 2, __, __, __, __, __
   "add 3"   0, __, __, __, __, __, __
   "add 4"   0, __, __, __, __, __, __
   "add 6"   0, __, __, __, __, __, __

   a. "add 2" and "add 4"
   b. "add 3" and "add 4"
   c. "add 2" and "add 6"
   d. "add 3" and "add 6"

4. In which place would the 5 be in the number that has a value 100 times the number below?

   50

   a. thousands place
   b. hundreds place
   c. tens place
   d. ones place

5. Use powers of 10 to represent the number four thousand.
   a. 4×10^2
   b. 4×10^3
   c. 4×10^4
   d. 4×10^5

6. Choose the number expressed by 5×10^5.
   a. 5,000
   b. 50,000
   c. 500,000
   d. 5,000,000

7. Expand 5,482.61 using place values.
   a. $5 \times 1,000 + 4 \times 100 + 8 \times 10 + 2 \times 1 + 6 \times \left(\frac{1}{10}\right) + 1 \times \left(\frac{1}{100}\right)$

   b. $5 \times 100 + 4 \times 10 + 8 \times 1 + 2 + 6 \times \left(\frac{1}{10}\right) + 1 \times \left(\frac{1}{100}\right)$

   c. $5 \times 1,000 + 4 \times 100 + 8 \times 10 + 2 \times 1 + 6 \times \left(\frac{1}{1}\right) + 1 \times \left(\frac{1}{10}\right)$

   d. $5 \times 10,000 + 4 \times 1,000 + 8 \times 100 + 2 \times 10 + 6 \times \left(\frac{1}{10}\right) + 1 \times \left(\frac{1}{100}\right)$

8. Choose the number expressed below:

   $2 \times 10,000 + 4 \times 1,000 + 6 \times 100 + 0 \times 10 + 3 \times 1 + 7 \times \left(\frac{1}{10}\right) + 9 \times \left(\frac{1}{100}\right)$.

   a. 2,463.79
   b. 20,463.79
   c. 24,063.79
   d. 24,603.79

9. Choose the number that completes the equation:

   $21,561.72 < $ ▪

   a. 21,560.72
   b. 21,571.72
   c. 21,461.72
   d. 21,561.71

10. Round 514,684.51 to the thousands place.
   a. 510,000.00
   b. 514,000.00
   c. 515,000.00
   d. 520,000.00

11. Multiply:

$$5,349$$
$$\times\ 24$$

    a. 32,094
    b. 128,376
    c. 138,576
    d. 224,658

12. Divide:

$$28\overline{)3584}$$

    a. 103
    b. 108
    c. 123
    d. 128

13. Which method below is NOT correct for finding the amount owed if three items are purchased at $3.99 each?
    a. $3 \times 4 - 3 \times 0.01$
    b. $3.99 \div 3$
    c. $3 \times 3 + 3 \times 0.9 + 3 \times 0.09$
    d. $3.99 + 3.99 + 3.99$

14. Add:

$$\frac{3}{5} + \frac{8}{11} =$$

    a. $\frac{1}{5}$

    b. $\frac{11}{16}$

    c. $1\frac{18}{55}$

    d. $1\frac{48}{55}$

15. At Sally's birthday party, 5 pizzas were ordered. The pepperoni pizza was cut into 8 slices and 6 pieces were eaten. The cheese pizza was cut into 12 slices and 9 pieces were eaten. The sausage pizza was cut into 6 slices and 6 pieces were eaten. The ham and pineapple pizza was cut into 8 slices and 4 pieces were eaten. The vegetable pizza was cut into 6 slices and 1 piece was eaten. How much pizza was left after the party?

   a. 1 pizza

   b. $1\frac{5}{6}$ pizzas

   c. 2 pizzas

   d. 4 pizzas

16. Where would the answer to $\frac{4}{5} - \frac{1}{16}$ lie on the number line below?

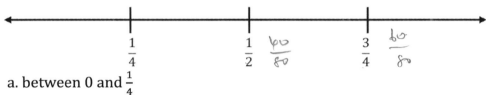

   a. between 0 and $\frac{1}{4}$

   b. between $\frac{1}{4}$ and $\frac{1}{2}$

   c. between $\frac{1}{2}$ and $\frac{3}{4}$

   d. between $\frac{3}{4}$ and 1

$$\frac{64}{80} - \frac{5}{80} = \frac{59}{80}$$

17. Bert has 4 dogs and 5 cans of dog food. How much dog food does each dog get if Bert gives each dog the same amount?

   a. $\frac{1}{2}$ of a can

   b. $\frac{4}{5}$ of a can

   c. 1 can

   d. $1\frac{1}{4}$ cans

18. At a sleepover, seven girls share 4 quarts of ice cream equally. How much ice cream does each girl eat?

  a. $\frac{1}{2}$ a quart

  b. $\frac{4}{7}$ a quart

  c. 1 quart

  d. $1\frac{3}{4}$ quarts

19. Every day for school, Henry's mom makes his lunch and gives him $\frac{3}{4}$ of a candy bar. At the end of the week, how many candy bars has she given Henry?

  a. 3 candy bars

  b. $3\frac{3}{4}$ candy bars

  c. 4 candy bars

  d. 5 candy bars

20. Find the area of a rectangle with length 3 in and width $\frac{3}{8}$ in by counting the number of $\frac{3}{8}$ in $\times$ $\frac{3}{8}$ in tiles needed to fill the rectangle.

$\frac{3}{8}$ in

3 in

$\frac{3}{8}$ in

$\frac{3}{8}$ in

  a. 8 tiles; $1\frac{1}{8}$ in²

  b. 3 tiles; 3 in²

  c. 8 tiles; 3 in²

  d. 3 tiles; $1\frac{1}{8}$ in²

21. Given that $487,956 \times 15 = 7,319,340$, which of the following is most likely the answer to $487,956 \times 24$?

  a. 5,345,204

  b. 6,597,004

  c. 7,051,454

  d. 11,710,944

22. Place the following in order from least to greatest, without computing the product:

$$\frac{3}{4} \times 1 \qquad\qquad \frac{3}{4} \times 0 \qquad\qquad \frac{3}{4} \times \frac{1}{4} \qquad\qquad \frac{3}{4} \times \frac{5}{4}$$

a. $\frac{3}{4} \times 0,\quad \frac{3}{4} \times \frac{1}{4},\quad \frac{3}{4} \times 1,\quad \frac{3}{4} \times \frac{5}{4}$

b. $\frac{3}{4} \times 0,\quad \frac{3}{4} \times \frac{1}{4},\quad \frac{3}{4} \times \frac{5}{4},\quad \frac{3}{4} \times 1$

c. $\frac{3}{4} \times 1,\quad \frac{3}{4} \times \frac{5}{4},\quad \frac{3}{4} \times \frac{1}{4},\quad \frac{3}{4} \times 0$

d. $\frac{3}{4} \times \frac{5}{4},\quad \frac{3}{4} \times 1,\quad \frac{3}{4} \times \frac{1}{4},\quad \frac{3}{4} \times 0$

23. A 42-in TV screen has length $20\frac{1}{2}$ in and width $36\frac{1}{2}$ in. What is the area of the viewing screen?

a. 114 in²

b. 720 in²

c. 748 in²

d. $748\frac{1}{4}$ in²

24. Divide:

$$\frac{1}{5} \div 3 =$$

a. $\frac{1}{7}$

b. $\frac{3}{15}$

c. 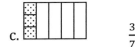 $\frac{3}{7}$

d. 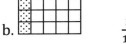 $\frac{1}{15}$

25. Choose the question that does NOT mean the same as the equation below:

$$2 \div \frac{1}{3} =$$

a. How many times does $\frac{1}{3}$ go into 2?

b. What is 2 divided by $\frac{1}{3}$?

c. How many times does 2 go into $\frac{1}{3}$?

d. What number times $\frac{1}{3}$ equals 2?

26. A family of five shares $\frac{1}{2}$ gallon of milk at breakfast. How much milk does each person get?

a. $\frac{1}{10}$ gallon

b. $\frac{1}{6}$ gallon

c. $\frac{1}{5}$ gallon

d. $\frac{5}{6}$ gallon

27. How many inches are in 15 feet?
a. 0.8 in
b. 1.25 in
c. 27 in
d. 180 in

28. The candy store has a new rope candy that costs $2.50 per foot. Jimmy has $12.50, how many inches of rope candy can he buy?
a. 5 in
b. 27 in
c. 60 in
d. 120 in

29. Nine friends have just finished their lunches. They notice that none of them finished their milk. Use the line plot below to find how much milk would be in each carton if the friends make all the milk levels even.

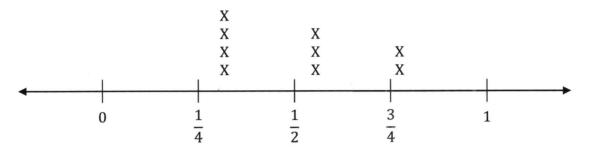

a. $\frac{1}{4}$ of a carton

b. $\frac{4}{9}$ of a carton

c. $\frac{1}{2}$ of a carton

d. $\frac{3}{4}$ of a carton

30. Which of the following is NOT a unit cube?

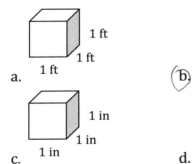

a. 1 ft, 1 ft, 1 ft

b. 2 mm, 2 mm, 2 mm

c. 1 in, 1 in, 1 in

d. 1 cm, 1 cm, 1 cm

31. How many unit cubes will fit inside the box below?

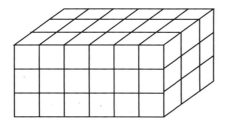

    a. 25 unit cubes
    b. 34 unit cubes
    c. 45 unit cubes
    d. 54 unit cubes

32. What is the volume of the solid below?

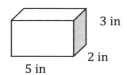

    3 in

    2 in

5 in

    a. 30 cubic inches
    b. 21 cubic inches
    c. 16 cubic inches
    d. 11 cubic inches

33. Which of the following is NOT a correct method to find the volume of a solid like the one below?

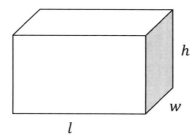

h

w

l

    a. Count the number of unit cubes in the solid
    b. Multiply the edge lengths: $V = l \times w \times h$
    c. Multiply the area of the base ($B = l \times w$) times the height: $V = B \times h$
    d. Add the edge lengths: $V = l + w + h$

34. What is the volume of a solid with a base with an area of 50 cm² and a height of 3 cm?
   a. 150 cubic cm
   b. 175 cubic cm
   c. 200 cubic cm
   d. 225 cubic cm

35. Find the volume of a solid with a length of 6 in, a width of 4 in, and a height of 10 in.
   a. 200 cubic inches
   b. 220 cubic inches
   c. 240 cubic inches
   d. 260 cubic inches

36. What is the volume of the solid below?

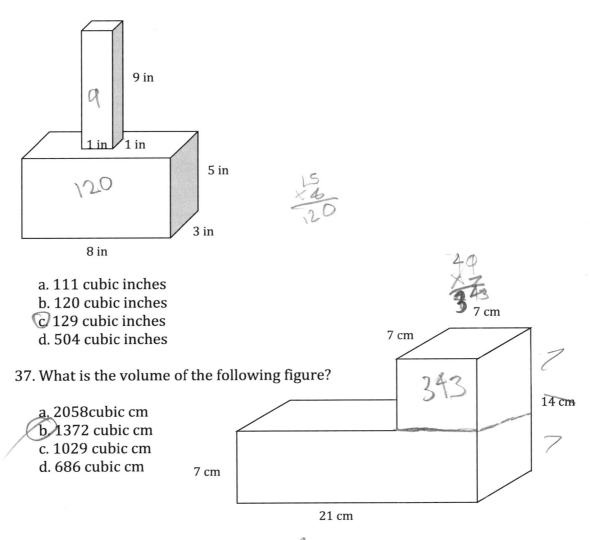

   a. 111 cubic inches
   b. 120 cubic inches
   c. 129 cubic inches
   d. 504 cubic inches

37. What is the volume of the following figure?

   a. 2058cubic cm
   b. 1372 cubic cm
   c. 1029 cubic cm
   d. 686 cubic cm

38. Choose the point located at (4,2).

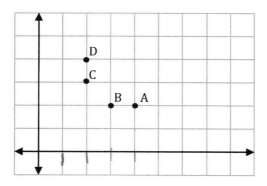

a. Point A
b. Point B
c. Point C
d. Point D

39. Choose the ordered pair that represents the location of the school on the map below.

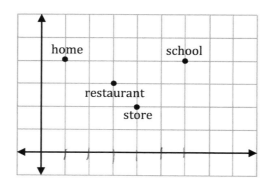

a. (1,4)
b. (3,3)
c. (4,2)
d. (6,4)

40. Use the graph below to determine how far the car has traveled after 5 hours.

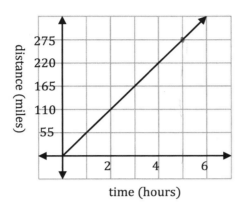

a. 220mi
b. 245mi
c. 260mi
d. 275mi

41. Parallelograms are four sided figures with two pairs of parallel sides. All of the following are parallelograms EXCEPT:

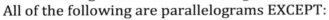

a. rectangle
b. trapezoid
c. square
d. rhombus

42. Choose the correct pair of words to complete the following statement.

All _____ triangles must be _____ triangles.

a. equilateral, acute
b. acute, scalene
c. obtuse, isosceles
d. scalene, right

Science

Learning about science is both fun and educational. The world is made up of all kinds of interesting plants and animals, in all shapes and sizes. We learn about these in science, and we also learn about things like stars and planets, weather, oceans, gravity, atoms, and much more. For many students, science is their favorite subject to study at school. Here are some questions about science that can help you improve your skills in this area.

Practice Test

Directions: Use the information below and your knowledge of science to answer questions 1 – 4.

The following is a "food web" showing the relationship among organisms in a certain ecosystem.

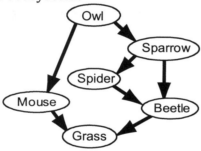

1. Which of the organisms shown is a primary consumer?
    a. Grass
    b. Mouse
    c. Owl
    d. Spider

2. The food web shows two organisms eating the grass, but it doesn't show the grass eating anything. Where does grass get its energy?
    a. Bacteria
    b. Sunlight
    c. Water
    d. Grass doesn't move, so it doesn't need energy.

3. Of which of the following organisms are there probably the *smallest number*?
   a. Beetles
   b. Mice
   c. Owls
   d. Sparrows

4. Important parts of the ecosystem not shown in this food web are the organisms, such as mushrooms, that feed on dead animals and plants and help break them down. What is the term for such organisms?
   a. Decomposers
   b. Herbivores
   c. Predators
   d. Producers

Directions: Use the information below and your knowledge of science to answer questions 5 – 8.

If you set a camera up pointing at the sky and leave it for a few hours, you can see how the stars appear to move across the sky over time. Here's an example of the kind of picture you can get:

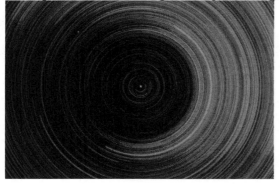

5. What exactly is causing the stars to appear to move?
   a. The rotation of the Earth around its axis
   b. The movement of the Earth around the Sun
   c. The movement of the Sun around the center of the galaxy
   d. It's not just apparent motion; the stars really do orbit the Earth.

6. If you look at the streak produced by any one star, you can see that it forms a semicircle. Based on that information, how much time passed while this picture was taken?
   a. One hour
   b. Two hours
   c. Four hours
   d. Twelve hours

7. What is the term for the motion of one object in the sky around another, such as the Earth around the Sun or the Moon around the Earth?
   a. Eclipse
   b. Gravity
   c. Orbit
   d. Solstice

8. The Sun is also a star, but it looks much bigger and brighter than other stars. What makes the Sun look so bright?
   a. The Sun is much larger than other stars.
   b. The Sun is much hotter than other stars.
   c. The Sun is much closer to the Earth than other stars.
   d. The Sun is pointed toward the Earth, whereas other stars are pointed away from the Earth.

Directions: Use the information below and your knowledge of science to answer questions 9 – 10.

When you mix together vinegar and baking soda, they form water, carbon dioxide, and a chemical called sodium acetate.

9. What is this is an example of?
   a. An atomic bomb
   b. A nuclear reaction
   c. A chemical analysis
   d. A chemical reaction

10. If you gathered together all the water, carbon dioxide, and sodium acetate that were produced, how would their combined weight compare to the weight of the vinegar and baking soda you started with?
   a. It would weigh more.
   b. It would weigh less.
   c. It would be equal.
   d. Carbon dioxide is a gas, so it doesn't have any weight.

Directions: Use the information below and your knowledge of science to answer questions 11 and 12.

A student puts a plant in a pot filled with soil, and then he levels the soil off. He sticks a ruler in the soil, touching the bottom of the pot, and he checks each week to see the level of the soil at the top of the ruler. Using another ruler, he also measures the height of the plant each week. He gets the following results:

	Dirt level	Height of plant
Week 1	18 cm	10 cm
Week 2	18 cm	15 cm
Week 3	18 cm	18 cm
Week 4	18 cm	20 cm
Week 5	18 cm	21 cm

11. Which of the following can be concluded from this experiment?
    a. Plants do not need soil to grow.
    b. The larger a plant grows, the more soil it needs.
    c. The pot didn't have enough soil for a healthy plant.
    d. The material for a plant's growth does not come mostly from the soil.

12. Which of the following would he have had to give the plant regularly to keep it growing?
    a. Charcoal dust
    b. Fertilizer
    c. Oil
    d. Water

13. What is soil made of, besides small particles of minerals (rock)?
    a. Tiny grains of dry ice, kept cold by insulation
    b. Organic materials from decomposed organisms
    c. The same chemicals that are found in Styrofoam
    d. Tiny bits of metal that boil up from the center of the Earth

14. Which of the following terms is used to collectively describe all of the living things on the Earth?
    a. Biosphere
    b. Exosphere
    c. Geosphere
    d. Thermosphere

15. What is the hydrosphere?
    a. The collective term for all the Earth's water
    b. The collective term for all the Earth's stone and mineral content
    c. The term for all the air surrounding the Earth
    d. The term for the part of outer space closer to the Earth than to any other planets

16. Which of the following describes one way in which the Earth's rocks and minerals can affect its air and climate?
    a. Rocks evaporate into the air and cause pollution.
    b. Mountains affect the motion of the air and wind patterns.
    c. Clouds are magnetically drawn to certain rocks, changing the air patterns.
    d. Continental drift can cause cyclones due to the motion of large parts of the Earth.

Directions: Use the information below and your knowledge of science to answer questions 17 – 20.

A student finds four metal blocks that are all the same size and have about the same appearance. He measures them all with the same instrument and records their weights in the following table.

	Weight
Block #1	35
Block #2	20
Block #3	50
Block #4	35

17. Based on his results, which of the blocks are most likely to be made of the same material?
    a. #1 and #2
    b. #3 and #4
    c. #1 and #4
    d. All of the blocks are probably made of the same material.

18. What important item did the student leave out of the table?
    a. The size of the blocks
    b. The units of the measurement
    c. The tenths place of the weights
    d. The leading zeros in the weights

19. Here, we were told that all the metal blocks looked similar, but if they were of different colors, would it still make sense to conclude that two of them were probably of the same material?

    a. Yes; based on his data, they still would probably have been the same material.

    b. No; color is another observation that can help distinguish between materials.

    c. Maybe; it depends on what colors they were.

    d. If the materials had different colors, he could not have obtained the results shown in the table.

20. In order to further test the similar blocks, the student decides to also measure another physical property, how easily they let electricity flow through them. What is this property called?

    a. Electrical conductivity

    b. Electrical resistance

    c. Electromagnetic force

    d. Thermal conductivity

Directions: Use the information below and your knowledge of science to answer questions 21 – 24.

One element that plays an important role in the biological processes of living things is *nitrogen*. Nitrogen is needed by plants and animals. Like other chemicals important for life, nitrogen goes through a cycle between living things and the environment. Although the atmosphere is made up mostly of nitrogen, most organisms cannot use the form of nitrogen that is in the air.

21. If plants cannot use the nitrogen in the air, where do they most likely get the nitrogen they need?

    a. From the soil

    b. From the Sun

    c. From the water

    d. From other plants

22. Where do most animals most likely get the nitrogen they need?

    a. From the soil

    b. From the Sun

    c. From the water

    d. From other organisms

23. What probably happens to the nitrogen of an organism when it dies?
    a. The nitrogen is lost forever.
    b. The nitrogen transforms into energy.
    c. The nitrogen transforms into some other element.
    d. The nitrogen is released back into the environment.

24. Besides chemicals such as nitrogen, what other important quantity is passed between organisms and their environment in a cycle?
    a. Energy
    b. Instinct
    c. Motion
    d. Time

Directions: Use the information below and your knowledge of science to answer questions 25 – 28.

The following pie chart shows the distribution of freshwater in the Earth.

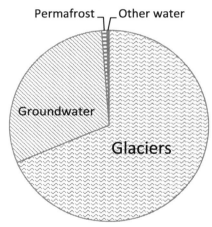

25. According to this chart, about how much of the Earth's freshwater is in lakes and rivers?
    a. 90%
    b. 65%
    c. 35%
    d. Less than 1%

26. One of the sections of the pie chart is labeled "Groundwater." What is groundwater?
    a. Water on the ground, such as in rivers and lakes
    b. Water that comes out of the ground, in springs and fountains
    c. Water that is underground, in and beneath the soil and rocks
    d. Water that is mixed with ground, or in other words, mud

27. Fifty thousand years ago, the Earth was in the middle of a glacial period during which much more of the Earth's surface was covered in glaciers than it is right now. How would a pie chart of the distribution of the freshwater on Earth fifty thousand years ago look different from the one above?
    a. The "Glaciers" section would be smaller, and the other sections would be larger.
    b. The "Glaciers" section would be larger, and the other sections would be smaller.
    c. The "Glaciers" section would be larger, overlapping the other sections, which would still be the same size.
    d. The pie chart would still look exactly the same as it does now.

28. There is 40 times as much saltwater as freshwater on the Earth. What would the pie chart above look like if it showed *all* the water, including saltwater?
    a. The saltwater would be put in a small sliver at the top.
    b. About half of the pie chart would show saltwater, and the other half would show the freshwater it shows now.
    c. Most of the pie chart would be taken up by the saltwater; all the sections in the current pie chart would be squeezed together into a thin slice.
    d. The pie chart would still look exactly the same as it does now.

Directions: Use the information below and your knowledge of science to answer questions 29 – 31.

Some of the first engines that didn't rely on human or animal power were steam engines, in which water is boiled and turned into steam that then interacts with the engine to generate energy. In one kind of steam engine, the steam turns rotating parts of the machine called turbines and generates energy, as shown in the simplified diagram below.

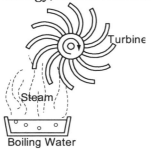

29. What state of matter is steam?
    a. Gas
    b. Liquid
    c. Solid
    d. Steam is not made of matter.

30. What is a scientific explanation for how the steam makes the turbine rotate?
    a. Steam is magnetically charged, so the turbine is attracted to it.
    b. The steam consists of many microscopic particles that hit the turbine and give it a push.
    c. Steam is not a physical substance, but it is composed of pure force that moves the turbine.
    d. The steam is an irrelevant by-product of the process; it's really just the heat that moves the turbine.

31. What happens to the steam after it passes by the turbine?
    a. The steam turns into air.
    b. The steam turns into energy.
    c. The steam disappears completely.
    d. The steam spreads out and is dispersed through the air.

32. What is the term for all the organisms of one species in a particular ecosystem?
    a. Biome
    b. Community
    c. Habitat
    d. Population

33. What is the term for a cold forest made up of pine trees and other conifers?
    a. Ice cap
    b. Prairie
    c. Taiga
    d. Tundra

34. Which of the following best describes a healthy ecosystem?
    a. An ecosystem with only one species
    b. An ecosystem with only two or three species
    c. An ecosystem with many species in stable relationships
    d. An ecosystem with many species in relationships that are constantly changing

35. A wealthy landowner is tired of all the flies that live in the area around his home, and he considers importing a foreign species of frog to eat the flies. Is this a good idea?
    a. Yes, because insects are bad for the ecosystem.
    b. No, because birds would be more effective at eating insects than frogs.
    c. Yes, because introducing more variety into an ecosystem is always good.
    d. No, because introducing a foreign species can damage the balance of an ecosystem.

36. One of the first people recorded to have reached the top of Mount Everest, more than five miles above sea level, was a Nepalese guide named Tenzing Norgay, who left some bars of mint cake on the peak. What direction did the Earth's gravity pull the mint cake?
    a. Up
    b. Down
    c. North
    d. South

37. In the deepest parts of the ocean, too deep for sunlight to reach, are hydrothermal vents that emit hot water filled with chemicals. Some bacteria feed on these chemicals, small crustaceans called copepods eat the bacteria, and snails and fish eat the small crustaceans. Certain deep-sea fungi there may break down dead organisms. Which of the organisms mentioned fulfills an ecological niche most similar to that of plants on land?

    a. The bacteria
    b. The copepods
    c. The snails and fish
    d. The fungi

Social Studies

Social studies classes cover many different topics. They include learning where people live, how they get along with each other, and how they organize their governments. Along with these subjects, students also learn about history, law, money, and religion, and how they have helped make different people groups what they are today. These social studies questions cover these topics and more, and will help you get more out of your classes.

Practice Test

1. Which branch of government has the authority to declare war?
    a. Judicial
    b. Legislative
    c. Executive
    d. Federal

2. According to the U.S. Constitution, how often is a census supposed to be performed in the United States?
    a. Every 5 years
    b. Every 7 years
    c. Every 10 years
    d. Every 20 years

3. Which of the following could be described as a want instead of a need?
    a. Vegetables
    b. Computer
    c. Medication
    d. Education

4. What is a group of islands called?
    a. Archipelago
    b. Atoll
    c. Estuary
    d. Isthmus

5. During a presidential election, citizens have the right to vote for the candidate of their choice. According to the U.S. Constitution, however, the final decision about who becomes president is made by what organization?
   a. House of Representatives
   b. Senate
   c. Supreme Court
   d. Electoral College

6. What type of landform is actually a large mass of slowly moving ice?
   a. Coral reef
   b. Glacier
   c. Fjord
   d. Levee

7. What was the original name of New York City?
   a. New Amsterdam
   b. Charles Town
   c. Fort Goede Hoop
   d. Fort Christina

8. Adam is an American citizen planning a visit to Brazil, and he needs to make sure he has the correct documentation for his trip. What document does he need, issued by the government of Brazil, that will allow him to enter the country?
   a. Credit card
   b. Visa
   c. Passport
   d. Boarding pass

9. During his farewell address, President George Washington warned the American people against what?
   a. Elections
   b. Congress
   c. Democracy
   d. Political parties

10. At the end of the year, Balfour Paper Company discovered that there was money left over in the budget. What is this extra money called?
   a. Capital
   b. Production
   c. Surplus
   d. Deficit

11. Which of the following would be considered a natural resource?
    a. Factory
    b. Forest
    c. Friendship
    d. Flute

12. Which of the following men, not a president, was the first chief justice of the Supreme Court?
    a. John Jay
    b. James Madison
    c. John Adams
    d. James Monroe

13. Harmon is starting a business and needs to find investors who are willing to take a risk on him. What is the term for the money that Harmon needs to get his business off the ground?
    a. Budget
    b. Asset
    c. Debt
    d. Capital

14. Which American announced, "I have not yet begun to fight!" during the Revolutionary War?
    a. Richard Henry Lee
    b. Patrick Henry
    c. James a. Garfield
    d. John Paul Jones

Directions: Use the map above and your knowledge of social studies to answer questions 15 through 17.

15. Based on the map, what would be considered the southernmost city in the state of New York?
    a. Jamestown
    b. New York
    c. Newburgh
    d. White Plains

16. Which lake lies to the east of the state of New York?
    a. Lake Champlain
    b. Lake Ontario
    c. Lake Erie
    d. Finger Lakes

17. Based on the map, what is the capital of New York?
    a. New York
    b. Troy
    c. Albany
    d. Rochester

18. In which year was the Declaration of Independence written?
   a. 1774
   b. 1775
   c. 1776
   d. 1777

19. What treaty ended the American Revolution?
   a. Treaty of Yorktown
   b. Treaty of Brussels
   c. Treaty of Paris
   d. Treaty of Breslau

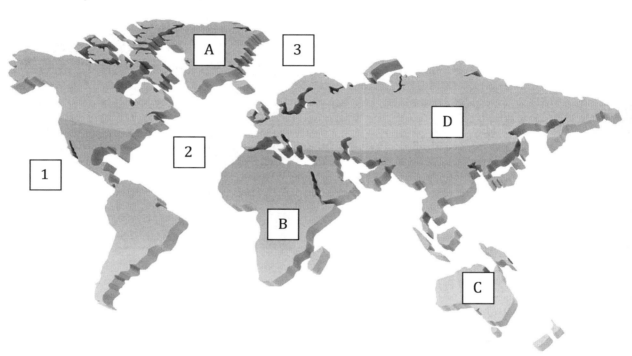

Directions: Use the map above and your knowledge of social studies to answer questions 20 through 22.

20. Which ocean is indicated by the number 2 above?
   a. Pacific Ocean
   b. Atlantic Ocean
   c. Arctic Ocean
   d. Indian Ocean

21. The Arctic Ocean is indicated by which number?
   a. 1
   b. 2
   c. 3
   d. 4

22. The continent that lies directly east of South America is indicated by which letter above?
   a. A
   b. B
   c. C
   d. D

23. The city of Deep River has struggled through a bad winter, and the roads are in bad shape. The money for these road repairs will be supplied largely by what?
   a. Assets
   b. Inflation
   c. Bartering
   d. Taxes

24. What is the term used for the molten rock that is produced by an erupting volcano?
   a. Quartz
   b. Lava
   c. Granite
   d. Shale

25. How many ratified amendments to the U.S. Constitution are there?
   a. 20
   b. 23
   c. 27
   d. 31

26. What percentage of the states must ratify an amendment to the U.S. Constitution before it can become law?
   a. 50
   b. 65
   c. 75
   d. 90

27. Which of the following would NOT be monitored by a state's Department of Natural Resources?
    a. Lakes
    b. Fish
    c. Wetlands
    d. Factories

28. Who was the president of the Confederacy during the Civil War?
    a. Robert E. Lee
    b. Jefferson Davis
    c. James Buchanan
    d. William T. Sherman

29. Which of the following rights is NOT granted in the Bill of Rights?
    a. Free speech
    b. Freedom to practice religion
    c. Women's vote
    d. Free press

30. Which mountain is the highest in the world?
    a. Kilimanjaro
    b. Matterhorn
    c. Etna
    d. Everest

31. Which battle began the Civil War?
    a. Fort Sumter
    b. Bull Run
    c. Shiloh
    d. Camp Allegheny

32. The Native American Sequoia, known for inventing an alphabet for his language, was a member of what tribe?
    a. Sioux
    b. Apache
    c. Cherokee
    d. Dakota

33. Which of the following continents is in both the Northern Hemisphere and the Southern Hemisphere?
    a. Asia
    b. Africa
    c. Australia
    d. Europe

34. Which group was fighting to end slavery in the United States?
    a. Protectionists
    b. Abolitionists
    c. Secessionists
    d. Sectionalists

35. To run for president of the United States, an individual must be at least how old?
    a. 32
    b. 34
    c. 35
    d. 37

36. To vote in an election, an individual must be how old?
    a. 16
    b. 18
    c. 21
    d. 25

37. What African-American woman is famous for refusing to move from her seat on the bus?
    a. Rosa Parks
    b. Phyllis Wheatley
    c. Harriet Tubman
    d. Sojourner Truth

Vocabulary

Words are powerful things. Just think about how much of your life revolves around words, whether they're spoken or written. Without words, life as we know it wouldn't exist, because communication with others is the foundation of society. Without words we couldn't learn, we couldn't read, we couldn't talk to our friends or family members. In fact, we couldn't communicate at all except for grunting and motioning at each other.

That's why it's important to have a large vocabulary. Your vocabulary is simply the entire group of words you know the meaning of. When you know a lot of words, the world opens up to you. You gain a deeper understanding of all aspects of life, and you become more successful in school. You make a better impression on others. When you work to build a good vocabulary, you'll be much better prepared to do well in college, and then in a career. The following exercise will help you improve your vocabulary.

Practice Test

For each sentence, choose the answer that is the closest in meaning to the word in italics.

1. It's *elementary*, my dear Watson.
   a. for people under age 13
   b. something that lasts all day
   c. something a person studies
   d. something basic

2. Let's hope it doesn't *revert*.
   a. get bigger
   b. become smaller
   c. go back
   d. go forward

3. Class, you've been so *diligent* lately.
   a. hard at work
   b. very quiet
   c. on time
   d. fun to be around

4. That's *absurd*, Thomas.
    a. wonderful
    b. hilarious
    c. nonsensical
    d. correct

5. I must stress the *urgency* of the situation.
    a. loudness
    b. violence
    c. requiring immediate action
    d. requiring a lot of money

6. Don't *scald* yourself.
    a. trip or cause to fall
    b. burn
    c. criticize
    d. take on too much responsibility

7. Did you *compensate* your workers?
    a. pay
    b. talk with
    c. fire
    d. observe

8. This item is *defective*.
    a. eye-catching
    b. perfect
    c. expensive
    d. faulty

9. Frankly, he seemed *reluctant*.
    a. confused
    b. unwilling
    c. rude
    d. eager

10. I've got my father's *consent*.
    a. money
    b. pocket watch
    c. permission
    d. house

11. Sally is in a *dismal* mood.
    a. excited
    b. sad
    c. happy
    d. angry

12. Once you pass the red barn, the trail begins to *descend*.
    a. go uphill
    b. go downhill
    c. get rougher
    d. get smoother

13. Did the holder of the winning raffle ticket *emerge*?
    a. go home
    b. turn up
    c. give it away
    d. share with everyone

14. This plant is *dormant* in the winter.
    a. inactive
    b. brought indoors
    c. decorated
    d. fast growing

15. I would like to *enlist*.
    a. quit
    b. sign up
    c. make a list
    d. lie down

16. The river is *murky*.
    a. very wide
    b. curved in spots
    c. dark and dirty
    d. fast moving

17. Your actions will lead to a *revolt*.
    a. rebellion
    b. argument
    c. electric shock
    d. new election

18. This computer is *obsolete*.
    a. brand new
    b. used
    c. out of date
    d. heavy

19. Can you get me a *duplicate*?
    a. helper
    b. exact copy
    c. colorful uniform
    d. a kind of dessert

20. They found a place of *refuge*.
    a. having lots of water
    b. where trash is taken
    c. being safe from danger
    d. where lots of plants grow

21. I'm going to take a *stroll*.
    a. umbrella
    b. kind of pastry
    c. wild guess
    d. short walk

22. This painting is very *significant*.
    a. important
    b. old
    c. colorful
    d. puzzling

23. How far is the *summit* from here?
    a. middle
    b. top
    c. bottom
    d. edge

24. That's an *approximate* number.
    a. having seven digits
    b. close but not exact
    c. negative
    d. written in Roman numerals

25. Did you *pursue* your dreams?
    a. achieve
    b. write down
    c. give up on
    d. follow

26. Where is the *document*?
    a. desk
    b. copy machine
    c. main office
    d. important paper

27. Please *proceed*.
    a. line up
    b. be quiet
    c. keep going
    d. stop

28. His *opponent* glared at him.
    a. rival
    b. teacher
    c. principal
    d. next door neighbor

29. We don't want to *exhaust* the kids.
    a. make angry
    b. make tired
    c. confuse
    d. wake up

30. You shouldn't be so *aggressive*.
    a. lazy
    b. shy; bashful
    c. eager to fight
    d. very loud

31. Don't *omit* anything.
    a. leave out
    b. give away
    c. say
    d. take

32. It has been *diluted*.
    a. thrown away
    b. weakened
    c. moved to another location
    d. sold

33. Some of my ancestors were *peasants* in the Middle Ages.
    a. princes
    b. rich bankers
    c. poor farmers
    d. priests

34. The *expedition* was successful.
    a. a journey to learn things
    b. a medical operation in a hospital
    c. a big conference where people discuss things
    d. the tearing down of an old building

35. He seemed very *nonchalant* about it.
    a. relaxed
    b. angry
    c. nervous
    d. frightened

36. Sometimes Edward can be a *nuisance*.
    a. good helper
    b. someone to talk to
    c. bothersome pest
    d. very smart person

37. Everyone on the team was *jubilant*.
    a. ready to play
    b. worn out
    c. very sad
    d. very happy

Spelling Practice

Being good at spelling is a skill that will be very important as you go through life. Sometimes when you're frustrated with it, it might seem as if good spelling skills are only useful in school, but nothing could be further from the truth. Being able to spell properly is something that will prove very useful nearly every day of your life, long after you have finished high school and even after you have graduated from college. Don't ever think spelling isn't important. It's actually very important, and you should always be working to get better at it.   exercise will test your spelling skills.

Practice Test

Spelling Exercise
Each question contains four words for you to consider. If one of them is misspelled, circle it. If they are all spelled correctly, circle NO MISTAKES.

1. simplicity	process	description	squonder	NO MISTAKES
2. retreve	account	membrane	query	NO MISTAKES
3. achieve	egzample	ceremony	recognize	NO MISTAKES
4. swetter	different	actually	tourist	NO MISTAKES
5. significance	companies	librery	represent	NO MISTAKES
6. calendar	businesses	garbage	divedend	NO MISTAKES
7. lether	politics	addict	routine	NO MISTAKES
8. pronounce	utensil	colum	pastry	NO MISTAKES
9. exhale	relatives	final	obblong	NO MISTAKES
10. route	incist	especially	despair	NO MISTAKES
11. proceed	feeture	difference	greatest	NO MISTAKES
12. define	nesesary	possible	chamber	NO MISTAKES

13. fragile	million	oxyjen	intolerant	NO MISTAKES
14. writer	ghetto	asimilate	prayer	NO MISTAKES
15. mountain	guitar	argument	fijet	NO MISTAKES
16. glare	clothes	accuse	ubstruct	NO MISTAKES
17. mithology	bought	capacity	guard	NO MISTAKES
18. ficility	courtesy	evening	advantage	NO MISTAKES
19. devotion	alltho	tornado	wanton	NO MISTAKES
20. galley	system	audience	icycle	NO MISTAKES
21. image	underline	obligate	domanant	NO MISTAKES
22. glory	quarter	brilliant	solow	NO MISTAKES
23. fatige	boundary	religion	president	NO MISTAKES
24. increese	advertisement	volunteer	supply	NO MISTAKES
25. eighth	toward	period	electric	NO MISTAKES
26. curtin	purpose	swerve	curve	NO MISTAKES
27. quartet	conscious	Mississippi	valyew	NO MISTAKES
28. texture	repair	colunny	thirtieth	NO MISTAKES
29. certificate	section	loyal	imperor	NO MISTAKES
30. recite	pateet	covet	pivot	NO MISTAKES

Capitalization

Some words need to be capitalized. For this reason, there are rules to help you remember which words need capitalization. Capitalizing can be confusing, so a good rule of thumb is that words are capitalized if they are unique persons, places or things (nouns), if they start a sentence, or if they are part of a person's or thing's title.

Some quick capitalization rules – all these should be capitalized:
- The first word of every sentence
- The first word of a quote
- Names of persons, months, days, holidays, countries, states, and cities
- Initials used in names and well-known organizations
- The word "I"
- Titles of books, songs, or people

Read each numbered item, and then decide if it's capitalized correctly, or incorrectly. If it's capitalized incorrectly, choose the answer which contains the mistake. If it's capitalized correctly, choose NO MISTAKES. Sentences may contain words that aren't capitalized that should be, or words that are capitalized that shouldn't be, or both.

1. Jenny and Kim want to have a Sleepover.
   a. Jenny and Kim
   b. want to have
   c. a Sleepover.
   d. NO MISTAKES

2. They have planned the party for friday Night.
   a. They have planned
   b. the party for
   c. friday Night.
   d. NO MISTAKES

3. "Let me know if your mom says we can have it at your house," said Kim.
   a. "Let me know if your
   b. mom says we can have it
   c. at your house," said Kim.
   d. NO MISTAKES

4. "She will, i am sure of it," replied Jenny.
    a. "She will, i am
    b. sure of it,"
    c. replied Jenny.
    d. NO MISTAKES

5. The next school Holiday is Thanksgiving.
    a. The next
    b. school Holiday
    c. is Thanksgiving.
    d. NO MISTAKES

6. Jenny's mom works as a secretary for a county judge.
    a. Jenny's mom works
    b. as a secretary for
    c. a county judge.
    d. NO MISTAKES

7. Her boss, judge Johnson, is very nice.
    a. Her boss,
    b. judge Johnson,
    c. is very nice.
    d. NO MISTAKES

8. Kim's favorite band is one Direction.
    a. Kim's favorite
    b. band is
    c. one Direction.
    d. NO MISTAKES

9. Our minister, reverend Brown, came over to visit.
    a. Our minister,
    b. reverend Brown, came
    c. over to visit.
    d. NO MISTAKES

10. Last night we watched the first star wars movie.
    a. Last night we
    b. watched the first
    c. star wars movie.
    d. NO MISTAKES

11. The doctor told me, "you should take one tablet daily."
    a. The doctor told me,
    b. "you should take
    c. one tablet daily."
    d. NO MISTAKES

12. The last day of December is also the last Day of the Year.
    a. The last day of
    b. December is also the
    c. last Day of the Year.
    d. NO MISTAKES

13. I heard that kroger is opening a new store in town.
    a. I heard that
    b. kroger is opening a
    c. new store in town.
    d. NO MISTAKES

14. I hope earth never gets invaded by Extraterrestrials!
    a. I hope earth
    b. never gets invaded
    c. by Extraterrestrials!
    d. NO MISTAKES

15. I love to sing battle hymn of the Republic.
    a. I love to sing
    b. battle hymn of
    c. the Republic.
    d. NO MISTAKES

16. Do you know what date easter falls on this year?
    a. Do you know what
    b. date easter falls
    c. on this year?
    d. NO MISTAKES

17. I think Central Elementary is the best Elementary School in the entire city.
    a. I think Central Elementary
    b. is the best Elementary School
    c. in the entire city.
    d. NO MISTAKES

18. Mom told us, "you can play Video Games after you do your homework."
    a. Mom told us, "you can
    b. play Video Games after
    c. you do your homework."
    d. NO MISTAKES

19. My friend got a new nintendo for his Birthday.
    a. My friend got
    b. a new nintendo
    c. for his Birthday.
    d. NO MISTAKES

20. Dad said uncle Bob is two years older than he is.
    a. Dad said uncle Bob
    b. is two years older
    c. than he is.
    d. NO MISTAKES

21. I have cousins in Ohio, Texas, and new York.
    a. I have cousins
    b. in Ohio, Texas,
    c. and new York.
    d. NO MISTAKES

22. I read People magazine at the Doctor's Office.
    a. I read People
    b. magazine at the
    c. Doctor's Office.
    d. NO MISTAKES

23. My grandmother makes a Roast Beef dinner every Sunday.
    a. My grandmother makes
    b. a Roast Beef dinner
    c. every Sunday.
    d. NO MISTAKES

24. I have practically memorized Harry Potter and the philosopher's stone.
    a. I have practically memorized
    b. Harry Potter and the
    c. philosopher's stone.
    d. NO MISTAKES

Punctuation

Ending Punctuation

Periods, Questions Marks and Exclamation Points

There are three main types of sentences: declarative, interrogative, and exclamatory. The ending punctuation you choose to put on a sentence changes the type of sentence it becomes.

- **Declarative sentences** make a statement. A **period (.)** is the correct ending punctuation for a declarative sentence.
- **Interrogative sentences** ask a question. A question mark (?) is the correct ending punctuation for an interrogative sentence.
- **Exclamatory sentences** express excitement or deep emotion. An **exclamation point (!)** is the correct ending punctuation for an exclamatory sentence.

Read the sentences below and decide if the sentence is making a statement, asking a question, or expressing emotion.

1. What time does the game start _____

2. I returned my books to the library _____

3. Mom is making your favorite dinner tonight _____

4. Jason, your house is on fire _____

5. Is Nate your best friend _____

6. I love you _____

7. Nick, can we play at your house _____

8. Mr. Kessler's store sells school supplies _____

9. Where is your bicycle _____

10. That boy stole my bicycle _____

Commas

Commas are punctuation, too. A comma (,) tells the reader to pause for a moment, but not to stop completely. There are lots of rules for commas, depending on the situation.

A Few Rules for Commas
- Commas separate a series of three or more words or phrases. (*She likes dolls, ponies, and kittens.*)
- Commas are used in dates between the day and year (*December 7, 1941*) and after the year if there is more to the sentence. (*On December 7, 1941, the Japanese attacked Pearl Harbor.*)
- Commas separate the name of a city and the name of its state or country (*Dallas, Texas*) or if there is more of the sentence after the state. (*We were in Dallas, Texas, last month.*)
- Commas separate two independent clauses before the coordinating conjunction. (*Sarah was hungry, yet nothing sounded good to eat.*)
- Commas separate a dependent clause from an independent clause at the beginning of a sentence. (*Due to a flash flood, we were not able to play street hockey.*)
- Commas separate additional information that could be removed from the sentence without changing its meaning. (*Joey, the boy in the third row, finished his homework.*)
- Commas show pauses in the sentence. (*Outside, the boxes were stacked in rows.*)
- Commas separate Yes and No and tag questions. (*Yes, I would like another piece of pie. No, thank you, I have had enough. It's true, isn't it?*)
- Commas separate direct quotes from the information that introduces or explains the quote. (*"Please don't forget to put your papers on my desk," said the teacher.*)
- Commas separate introductory phrases of four or more words. (*At the end of the month, we will meet our quota.*)

Write the following sentences correctly by adding commas where they belong.

1. In Houston Texas there is a huge rodeo in February.

2. Johnny said "Let's go play on the swings."

3. It's going to rain today isn't it?

4. Nate had three apples two oranges and a banana in his lunch box.

5. Eureka a show on the SyFy channel is about a town of geniuses.

6. The Revolutionary War officially ended on May 12 1784.

7. Yes thank you I would love some cake.

8. Along with his friends Evan thought he could help others.

9. Because of the lightning we could not play outside.

10. We can vacation at the beach or we can go to the city.

Write two sentences of your own about music. Use a series in one sentence and a date in the other.

11. _____

_____

_____

_____

_____

12. _____

_____

_____

_____

_____

Titles

Titles can be confusing. Sometimes they are underlined, sometimes in italics, and sometimes in quotation marks.

Rules for Titles:
- Short works (such as the title of an article or a short poem) and parts of longer works (such as the title of a chapter) are usually in quotation marks. (*Title of a short story, "Young Goodman Brown"*)
- Long works (such as books, movies, television series, or albums) and collections of works (magazines, newspapers, anthologies) are placed in italics. You also can underline INSTEAD of using italics, but not both together. (Title of a Television series*: <u>iCarly</u> or* Title of a movie*: Star Wars Episode I)*

Punctuate the titles in the sentences below correctly by using quotations marks or by underlining.

1. To Kill a Mockingbird is my favorite novel.

2. The headline read, Man Kills Seven in Subway.

3. My class went to see An Ideal Husband, a play by Oscar Wilde.

4. The Avengers was the best movie this summer!

5. What Sarah Said, by Death Cab for Cutie, is the best song ever.

Practice Test Answers and Explanations

Reading

Living on a Ranch
1. C - The Bar M Bar Ranch is in Laramie, Wyoming
2. D - Marcus uses whistles and calls.
3. B - Marcus enjoys working with the sheep.
4. A - Everyone has a job on a ranch.
5. C - She is in charge of the household and bills.
6. B - Working and living on a ranch is a full time job.
7. B - People who work on a ranch owned by someone else.
8. A - They all help with chores on the ranch.

Geocaching
1. C - He always had fun when he was with Tommy and Mr. Jones.
2. A - The GPS was accurate only to 15 feet.
3. C - wool socks, hiking boots, and a backpack
4. A - Geocaching is a treasure hunt for small containers using GPS coordinates.
5. B - small items or toys to trade
6. D - Yes, Tommy teaches Sam about marking off a search area.
7. B - two friends going Geocaching with Mr. Jones
8. D - a hiding place

Dance Class
1. A - They want to learn to dance.
2. C - Jillian loves ballet, and Samantha loves tap.
3. D - Both classrooms have wooden floors and mirrors.
4. C - a classical type of dance
5. D - a bar on the wall for stretching
6. B - how much the sisters loved dance

Animals of Yellowstone
1. D - He wanted to know where to look for the animals.
2. A - South Entrance and West Thumb
3. B - Elk
4. C - More animals live in forests and meadows.
5. D - an animal's home area
6. B - The wolves have the smallest population.

A Day in the City

1. D - subway
2. C - Which subway lines would you take to get to the National Archives?
3. B - They enjoy doing things together.
4. C - The White House and the National Air and Space Museum
5. A – Definition 1. - A sheet arranging information into columns or tabs
6. A - It is only on one subway line.

Family Names

1. C - to explain family names based on occupation
2. A - to move people or things
3. D - definitions and origins of occupational words
4. B - was a chef.
5. A - Fletcher and Bender
6. C - Last name

Meteor Watching

1. C - The Perseid meteor shower is a favorite.
2. A - It only happens in August.
3. C - scattered fragments of rock
4. D - The Earth takes one year to orbit the sun, and the comet takes 135 years to orbit the sun.
5. B - People enjoy watching the shower because it happens in the summer.
6. B - average

Written Expression

Prepositions
1. between
2. over
3. across
4. toward
5. around

Conjunctions
1. and - coordinating
2. because - subordinating
3. Neither/nor - correlative
4. although - subordinating
5. not only / but also - correlative
6. but - subordinating
7. and - coordinating
8. Either / or - correlative
9. unless - subordinating
10. Both / and - correlative

Verb Tenses
1. will go - C
2. cooks - A
3. rained - B
4. will visit - C
5. lives - A
6. rode
7. enjoys
8. will read
9. wanted
10. will play

Changing Sentences
1. Nate and Evan go to the Houston Zoo on Sundays.
2. Dragonflies live by the river, where I hope to see some today.
3. Evan likes the monkeys that live in the primate habitat.
4. Baboons are from African and Asia, but they mostly live in zoos now.
5. Nick watches the baby giraffe as it tries to eat leaves from a tall tree.

Homophones
1. two
2. right
3. there
4. one
5. threw
6. err
7. aisle
8. ate
9. bass
10. bare

Heteronyms
1. The Polish furniture needs <u>polish</u>. (a substance to give a shiny surface)
2. I <u>object</u> to that object. (disapprove)
3. She was close enough to the window to <u>close</u> it. (to shut)
4. The bass drum had a <u>bass</u> painted on it. (a fish)
5. Mr. Jones is ready to <u>present</u> the present to the President. (to give formally)
6. Don't <u>desert</u> us just because we are in the desert. (to leave)
7. The <u>dove</u> dove for the food. (a bird)
8. Give me a minute and I'll show you <u>minute</u> particles in my microscope. (tiny)
9. The singer is here to <u>record</u> a new record. (to preserve in sound)
10. I <u>refuse</u> to take out the refuse. (to say no)

Greek / Latin
1.   A. photogenic
      B. photograph
      C. telephoto
      D. photosynthesis

2.   A. aerodynamics
      B. aerobics
      C. aerate
      D. aeronautics

3.   A. epidemic
      B. democracy
      C. demographic
      D. endemic

Context Clues

1. A - moved
2. B - get rid of
3. D - denied
4. A - huge
5. C - calm

Reference Materials

1. B - (2) /ˈmin(ē)əCHər/
2. C - (3)adj. of a much smaller size than normal
      noun. a thing that is much smaller than normal
      verb. represent on a smaller scale

3. D - (4)synonyms: diminutive, tiny, small
4. A - (1) Miniature
5. D - Encyclopedia
6. A - Dictionary
7. C - Thesaurus
8. B - Glossary

Figurative language

1. A - simile
2. D - onomatopoeia
3. E - idiom
4. B - metaphor
5. C - alliteration

Synonyms

1. big
2. hard
3. bucket
4. mad
5. talk

Antonyms

6. city
7. full
8. beautiful / pretty
9. thaw
10. catch

Mathematics

1. A: When expressions have braces, brackets, parentheses, begin on the inside and work out. Always work from left to right.

divide 4 by 2	$\{5 \times [9 - (4 \div 2) - 5]\} + 11 =$
subtract 2 from 9	$\{5 \times [9 - 2 - 5]\} + 11 =$
subtract 5 from 7	$\{5 \times [7 - 5]\} + 11 =$
multiply 5 by 2	$\{5 \times 2\} + 11 =$
add 10 and 11	$10 + 11 =$
	21

2. C: When subtraction comes before division, it must be placed in parentheses. The phrase "subtract 4 from 18" means the same as "18 minus 4."

3. C: The first seven terms of the sequence "add 2" are 0, 2, 4, 6, 8, 10, 12 and the first seven terms of the sequence "add 6" are 0, 6, 12, 18, 20, 24, 30, 36. Each of the terms in the "add 6" sequence is three times the corresponding term in the "add 2" sequence.

"add 2" sequence	"add 2" sequence times 3	"add 6" sequence
0	$0 \times 3 = 0$	0
2	$2 \times 3 = 6$	6
4	$4 \times 3 = 12$	12
6	$6 \times 3 = 18$	18
8	$8 \times 3 = 24$	24
10	$10 \times 3 = 30$	30
12	$12 \times 3 = 36$	36

4. A: $100 \times 50 = 5000$, so the 5 would be in the thousands place.

5. B: Four thousand is written 4,000. Count the zeros to find the exponent.

6. C: The exponent 5 means there are 5 zeros in the answer.

7. A: 5 is in the thousands place, 4 is in the hundreds place, 8 is in the tens place, 2 is in the ones place, 6 is in the hundredths place, and 1 is in the thousandths place.

8. D: 0×10 means a 0 must be written in the tens place.

9. B: All the other numbers are smaller than 21,561.72, but 21,571.72 is 10 more than 21,561.72.

10. C: To round to the thousands place, look at the digit to the right (in the hundreds place). If that digit is 4 or less, leave the digit in the thousands place; if that digit is 5 or more, add one to the digit in the thousands place.

11. B: Multiply 4 times 5,349. Then multiply 20 times 5,349. Finally, add the two numbers together.

$$
\begin{array}{r}
5,349 \\
\times\ 24 \\
\hline
21,396 \\
+106,980 \\
\hline
128,376
\end{array}
$$

12. D: Find the number of times 28 goes into 35; record this result (1) above the 5. Subtract 28 (28×1) from 35 and bring down the 8. Find the number of times 28 goes into 78; record this result (2) above the 8. Subtract 56 (28×2) from 78 and bring down the 4. Find the number of times 28 goes into 224; record this result (8) above the 4. Subtract 224 (28×8) from 224.

$$
\begin{array}{r}
128 \\
28\overline{)3584} \\
-28 \\
\hline
78 \\
-56 \\
\hline
224 \\
-224 \\
\hline
0
\end{array}
$$

13. B: Since 3 items are being purchased and each costs $3.99, these two numbers must be multiplied. Choice A shows $3 \times 4 - 3 \times 0.01 = 3 \times (4 - 0.01) = 3 \times 3.99$. Choice C shows $3 \times 3 + 3 \times 0.9 + 3 \times 0.09 =$

$3 \times (3 + 0.9 + 0.09) = 3 \times 3.99$. Choice D shows $3.99 + 3.99 + 3.99 = 3 \times 3.99$. Only choice B shows a different operation: division.

14. C: To add fractions with unlike denominators, a least common denominator must be found. For these two fractions, the LCD is $5 \times 11 = 55$. Both the numerator and denominator of the first fraction must be multiplied by 11 $\left(\frac{3 \times 11}{5 \times 11} = \frac{33}{55}\right)$) and both the numerator and denominator of the second fraction must be multiplied by 5 $\left(\frac{8 \times 5}{11 \times 5} = \frac{40}{55}\right)$). Now the fractions can be added by finding the sum of the two numerators $\left(\frac{33}{55} + \frac{40}{55} = \frac{73}{55}\right)$). Because this is an improper fraction, the fraction must be rewritten as a whole number and a proper fraction. 55 goes into 73 once (so 1 is the whole number) and the remainder is $73 - 55 = 18$ (so the proper fraction is $\frac{18}{55}$).

15. B:
Find the fraction of pizza left over from each pizza.

PIZZA:	pepperoni	cheese	sausage	ham and pineapple	vegetable
eaten:	$\frac{6}{8}$	$\frac{9}{12}$	$\frac{6}{6}$	$\frac{4}{8}$	$\frac{1}{6}$
left over:	$\frac{2}{8} = \frac{1}{4}$	$\frac{3}{12} = \frac{1}{4}$	0	$\frac{4}{8} = \frac{1}{2}$	$\frac{5}{6}$

Find the least common denominator.
$$\frac{1}{4} + \frac{1}{4} + \frac{1}{2} + \frac{5}{6} = \frac{1 \times 3}{4 \times 3} + \frac{1 \times 3}{4 \times 3} + \frac{1 \times 6}{2 \times 6} + \frac{5 \times 2}{6 \times 2} = \frac{3}{12} + \frac{3}{12} + \frac{16}{12} + \frac{10}{12}$$
Add the four fractions together.
$$\frac{3}{12} + \frac{3}{12} + \frac{16}{12} + \frac{10}{12} = \frac{22}{12}$$
Find the mixed number.
$$\frac{22}{12} = 1\frac{10}{12} = 1\frac{10 \div 2}{12 \div 2} = 1\frac{5}{6}$$

16. C: First, find the least common denominator: $\frac{4 \times 16}{5 \times 16} - \frac{1 \times 5}{16 \times 5} = \frac{64}{80} - \frac{5}{80}$, then subtract the numerators: $\frac{64}{80} - \frac{5}{80} = \frac{59}{80}$. To find where this answer lies on the number line, consider that $0 = \frac{0}{80}$, $\frac{1}{4} = \frac{20}{80}$, $\frac{1}{2} = \frac{40}{80}$, $\frac{3}{4} = \frac{60}{80}$, and $1 = \frac{80}{80}$. So $\frac{59}{80}$ is between $\frac{40}{80} = \frac{1}{2}$ and $\frac{60}{80} = \frac{3}{4}$.

17. D: The answer is found by dividing the number of cans by the number of dogs: $\frac{5 \text{ cans}}{4 \text{ dogs}}$. The fraction is improper, so rewrite it as a mixed number: 4 goes

into 5 once (so the whole number is 1) and the remainder is $5 - 4 = 1$ (so the numerator of the fraction is 1).

18. B: The answer is found by dividing the number of quarts by the number of girls: $\frac{4 \text{ quarts}}{7 \text{ girls}}$.

19. B: Henry ate $\frac{3}{4}$ of a candy bar for 5 days. To find the total number of candy bars, multiply $\frac{3}{4} \times 5 = 3 \times 5 \div 4 = \frac{15}{4} = 3\frac{3}{4}$.

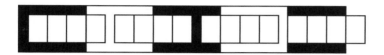

Monday   Tuesday   Wednesday   Thursday   Friday

20. A:

$\frac{3}{8}$ in

3 in

Each tile has an area of $\frac{3}{8} \times \frac{3}{8} = (3 \times 3) \div (8 \times 8) = \frac{9}{64}$ in². There are 8 tiles, so the area of the rectangle
is $\frac{9}{64} \times 8 = 9 \times 8 \div 64 = \frac{72}{64} = \frac{9}{8} = 1\frac{1}{8}$ in².
Multiplying the length and the width gives the same answer: $\frac{3}{8} \times 3 = 3 \times 3 \div 8 = \frac{9}{8} = 1\frac{1}{8}$ in².

21. D: Since 24 is larger than 15, the answer to $487,956 \times 24$ must be larger than the answer to $487,956 \times 15$.

22. A: When a fraction is multiplied by 0, the result is zero. When a fraction is multiplied by 1, the result is the same fraction. When a fraction is multiplied by a fraction between 0 and 1, the result is between 0 and the same fraction. When a fraction is multiplied by a fraction larger than 1, the result is larger than the fraction.

23. D: The area is found by multiplying $20\frac{1}{2} \times 36\frac{1}{2} = \frac{41}{2} \times \frac{73}{2} = \frac{2993}{4} = 748\frac{1}{4}$ in².

24. D: All 5 of the pieces must be cut into 3, creating 15 equal sections. The answer can be verified using multiplication: $\frac{1}{15} \times 3 = 1 \times 3 \div 15 = \frac{3}{15} = \frac{1}{5}$.

25. C: Choices A and B are based on division, with the correct divisor and dividend. Choice D is based on multiplication, the opposite of division, using the given numbers as one of the factors and the product. Only choice C is incorrect because it has the divisor and dividend confused.

26. A: Each family member is taking $\frac{1}{5}$ of the $\frac{1}{2}$ gallon. That divides the whole gallon into 10 parts, so each family member gets $\frac{1}{10}$ of a gallon. The answer can be verified using multiplication: $\frac{1}{10} \times 5 = 1 \times 5 \div 10 = \frac{5}{10} = \frac{1}{2}$.

27. D: To convert from feet to inches, multiply by the factor $\frac{12\ \text{in}}{1\ \text{ft}}$: $15\ \text{ft} \times \frac{12\ \text{in}}{1\ \text{ft}} = 180$ in.

28. C: $\$12.50 \times \frac{1\ \text{ft}}{\$2.50} \times \frac{12\ \text{in}}{1\ \text{ft}} = (12.50 \div 2.50) \times 12\ \text{in} = 5 \times 12\ \text{in} = 60$ in.

29. B: First, find the total amount of milk in the cartons: $4 \times \frac{1}{4} + 3 \times \frac{1}{2} + 2 \times \frac{3}{4} = 1 + \frac{3}{2} + \frac{6}{4} = \frac{2}{2} + \frac{3}{2} + \frac{3}{2} = \frac{8}{2} = 4$ cartons of milk. Then, divide the amount of milk by the number of cartons: $\frac{4}{9}$.

30. B: A unit cube must have side lengths of 1 unit. Since choice B has side lengths of 2 mm, it cannot be a unit cube.

31. D: There are 18 unit cubes on the front of the box, so the middle and the back will also have 18 unit cubes each. $18 \times 3 = 54$ unit cubes.

32. A: To find the volume, draw the unit cubes in to see that there are 5 across, 2 deep, and 3 up and down. Then count the number of cubes. There are 15 on the front and a matching 15 on the back: $15 + 15 = 30$ cubic inches.

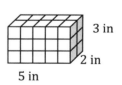
3 in
2 in
5 in

33. D: Choices A, finding the number of unit cubes that fit inside the solid, B, multiplying the side lengths, and C, multiplying the area of the base times the height, will give the same result: the volume. Choice D, adding the side lengths will not result in the volume.

34. A: $V = B \times h = 50 \times 3 = 150$ cubic centimeters.

35. C: $V = l \times w \times h = 6 \times 4 \times 10 = 240$ cubic inches.

36. C: $V_{top} = l \times w \times h = 1 \times 1 \times 9 = 9$ and $V_{bottom} = l \times w \times h = 8 \times 3 \times 5 = 120$. Volume is additive, so adding the two individual volumes will result in the total volume: $V_{top} + V_{bottom} = 9 + 120 = 129$ cubic inches.

37. B: $V_{top} = l \times w \times h = 7 \times 7 \times 7 = 343$ and $V_{bottom} = l \times w \times h = 21 \times 7 \times 7 = 1029$. Volume is additive, so adding the two individual volumes will result in the total volume: $V_{top} + V_{bottom} = 343 + 1029 = 1372$ cubic centimeters.

38. A: Point A is located at (4,2), the point four units to the right of the origin and two units above the origin.

39. D: The school is located six units to the right of the origin and four units above the origin, at (6,4).

40. D: Find the ordered pair with 5 as the x-value that lies on the line. The y-value of that ordered pair is 275.

41. B: A trapezoid has only one pair of parallel sides. A square, a rectangle, and a rhombus all have two pairs of parallel sides.

42. A: All equilateral triangles have three equal sides and three equal angles. The measure of those angles is 60°, so those angles can only be acute.

Science

1. B: A *primary consumer* is an organism that eats *producers*, which do not feed on other organisms and which form the bottom of the food web. In this case, the grass is the producer, and so the primary consumers are the organisms that eat the grass. Of the answer choices, the only one that eats grass is the mouse.

2. B: Even though it doesn't move, grass still needs energy to grow and develop. The energy that sustains grass and other green plants comes from the Sun, which provides energy through a process called photosynthesis. Although plants do need water, they use it for growth, not for energy.

3. C: Usually as you move up a food web, there are fewer organisms at each higher level. If sparrows eat beetles, for instance, then there are likely to be a lot more beetles than sparrows. There may be exceptions if, for instance, there is a particularly rare species of beetle, but then there must be other more numerous organisms at the same level on the food web to supply enough food for the higher levels. In any case, it's likely that there are the smallest numbers of the organisms highest up on the food web, which in this case are owls.

4. A: Organisms such as mushrooms and many bacteria that break up dead matter are called *decomposers*. An *herbivore* is an animal that eats plants, a *predator* is an organism that preys on other organisms, and a *producer* is an organism that produces energy from its environment (such as most plants).

5. A: The stars appear to move across the sky because of the Earth's rotation around its axis. To a person on the Earth, the Earth seems motionless and it appears that the stars are moving around the Earth. (Which stars are visible in the sky does change over time because of the Earth's rotation around the Sun, but that would happen on a time scale of months, not hours.)

6. D: Because it's the rotation of the Earth that makes the stars appear to move, they will take one day—the amount of time it takes the Earth to rotate once—to make a complete circle. Therefore, they will appear to go around half a circle in half a day. Because there are 24 hours in a day, half of a day is 12 hours.

7. C: When an object moves around another object such as the Earth around the Sun or the Moon around the Earth, it is said to *orbit* it: the Earth orbits the Sun, and the Moon orbits the Earth. *Orbit* can also be a noun: the path of the orbiting object is known as its orbit. An *eclipse* is a phenomenon that

occurs when one celestial object blocks the light from another—the best known kind of eclipse is a *solar eclipse*, when the Moon blocks the Sun from our view. A *solstice* is the time of year when the days are longest (as in the summer solstice) or shortest (as in the winter solstice). *Gravity* is the force by which objects draw each other together; the Earth orbits the Sun and the Moon orbits the Earth *because* of gravity, but it's not correct to say that gravity is the term for their motion.

8. C: Stars vary widely in their size, their temperature, and their distance from the Earth. There are many stars hotter than the Sun, and there are many stars larger than the Sun. However, the Sun is much closer to the Earth than any other star: the Sun is approximately 90 million miles away (about 150 million kilometers), and the next nearest star is more than a hundred thousand times as far away. As for being pointed toward the Earth, stars radiate light and heat in all directions; it doesn't really make sense to say a typical star is pointed in any particular direction.

9. D: When you mix together two chemicals and they recombine into different chemicals, this is called a *chemical reaction*.

10. C: In a chemical reaction, the total weight of the chemicals doesn't change. The weight of the chemicals you end up with is the same as the weight of the chemicals you start with. It's true that carbon dioxide is a gas, but gases do have weight.

11. D: The most significant thing to note from this experiment is that as the plant grows, the level of soil in the pot does not go down. This indicates that the plant is not getting much of the material for its growth from the soil. The material for a plant's growth comes mostly from the air and water.

12. D: Water is necessary for plants to grow. Even plants living in dry areas, such as cacti, need some water to be able to grow (cacti have many adaptations to allow them to conserve water, so they can get by with less water than other plants, but they still do need some water). Fertilizer can help plants grow faster, but it's not necessary.

13. B: When organisms die and decompose, they return some of their chemical content to the soil. Although it's not impossible for soil to contain grains of metal, this metal certainly wouldn't have "boiled up" from the center of the Earth (which doesn't really make sense; the metal at the center of the Earth is kept there by gravity, and it is melted but not boiling). The soil does not usually contain dry ice (dry ice is frozen carbon dioxide, and even the polar regions are not cold enough to keep carbon dioxide frozen) nor

does it contain the chemicals used to make Styrofoam (mostly a chemical called polystyrene, which is artificially created).

14. A: The *biosphere* is the collective term for all of the life on Earth. (The *exosphere* and the *thermosphere* are layers of the atmosphere, and the *geosphere* is the term for all the rocks and minerals in the Earth.)

15. A: The *hydrosphere* is the collective term for all of the water on the Earth's surface, including the water in the oceans, seas, lakes, and rivers as well as the water in clouds and rain, and even the ice in glaciers and icebergs. The term for the air around the Earth is the *atmosphere*, and all the Earth's rocks and minerals make up the *geosphere*. (There is no particular term for the part of outer space closer to the Earth than to other planets.)

16. B: The position of mountains may affect the wind patterns, which can have a strong effect on the climate. For instance, the air often has much more moisture on one side of mountains than the other because mountains slow down and cool the air moving across them and cause it to drop moisture on that side. Rocks do not evaporate (at least, not at temperatures found on the surface of the Earth); clouds are not magnetically drawn to rocks; and although continental drift does involve the movement of large amounts of rock, it is a very slow process, certainly much too slow to cause cyclones.

17. C: Different materials have different physical properties, including weight. (The weight also depends on how big the object is, of course, but here we're told the blocks are all the same size.) Because blocks A and D have the same weight, they are the ones most likely to be made of the same material.

18. B: For a measurement of weight or of another physical quantity to be meaningful, it must have *units*. From the student's data, we don't know whether these weights were measured in pounds, ounces, grams, kilograms, or some more obscure unit; he should have included the units of measurement. Although the size of the blocks may be an interesting datum to note, it's not directly relevant to what he's trying to measure, and it doesn't need to be in the table. It's also not a universal rule that weights have to be measured to the tenths place; there's nothing wrong with ending at the ones place (or with not including leading zeros).

19. B: Color is another physical property of materials that can be used to distinguish between them. If all of the blocks had different colors, they would probably have all been of different materials, even if two of them had the same weight.

20. A: A measurement of how easily an object lets electricity flow through it is called its *electrical conductivity*. *Electrical resistance* is a measurement of how much an object *restricts* the flow of electricity through it; it's the reciprocal of electrical conductivity. *Electromagnetic force* is a term for the fundamental force related to electricity, and *thermal conductivity* is a measurement of how well an object conducts *heat*, not electricity.

21. A: If plants do not get nitrogen from the air, they must get it from some other part of their environment. They can't get it from water, because water is H_2O; it contains only hydrogen and oxygen. They can't get it from sunlight, because sunlight only gives energy; it doesn't contain any chemicals. They can't get it from other plants, because plants don't eat each other. The only place left for them to get it from is the soil. (There are bacteria that take nitrogen from the air and put it in the soil in a form useful to plants. These bacteria live in the roots of certain plants, such as peas, so it's sometimes said that these plants put nitrogen in the soil, even though it's really the bacteria living in the roots that are doing it.)

22. D: Unlike plants, animals don't use chemicals from the soil directly. However, unlike most plants, animals *do* eat other organisms. They get their nitrogen from the organisms they eat—herbivores get it from the plants they eat, and carnivores get it from the other animals they eat. (There are some plants that *do* eat other organisms, such as the Venus fly trap; these plants often live in areas where the soil is poor in nitrogen and other essential nutrients, and they do get nitrogen from the animals they eat.)

23. D: When an organism dies, all the chemical content in its body is released back into the environment. Elements do not transform completely into energy, and elements do not transform into other elements except in a nuclear reaction or by radioactive decay.

24. A: Energy is transferred between different organisms and between organisms and their environment. Plants get energy from the Sun; animals get energy from the plants they eat; organisms that die leave behind chemical energy that returns to the environment. There is no meaningful sense in which instinct, motion, or time could be said to cycle between organisms and their environments.

25. D: Lakes and rivers are certainly not glaciers, nor are they groundwater (which refers to the water in the soil and underground). They're also not permafrost. They must therefore be included in the tiny sliver labeled "Other water," which is so thin it's definitely less than 1% of the total. All the Earth's lakes and rivers together hold less than 1% of the freshwater on the planet.

26. C: Groundwater is water that is underground. Some groundwater flows through cracks in rocks, some groundwater exists between grains of soil, and some groundwater lies in immobile deposits. Groundwater eventually does flow out through springs or into swamps and other wet areas, and it is replenished by rainwater soaking into the ground.

27. B: If more of the Earth's freshwater was in glaciers fifty thousand years ago, then the "Glaciers" section of the pie chart would be larger. This means the other sections would be smaller; sections of a pie chart cannot overlap.

28. C: If there is 40 times as much saltwater as freshwater, then the saltwater will take up 40 times the area on the chart. All the freshwater will be squeezed into a small slice. The graph might look something like this:

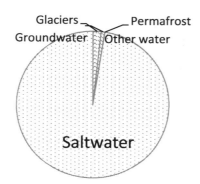

(In fact, this accurately represents the distribution of the Earth's water; 96.5% of the Earth's water is in the oceans, and another 0.9% is in other saltwater bodies. Most of the Earth's water is saltwater.)

29. A: Steam is a gas, like air and helium. We know it is a gas because it does not have a fixed volume; steam will expand to fill the area where it is. (Water is a liquid, of course, but when it is boiled it turns into a gas, steam.)

30. B: Like all gases, steam consists of microscopic particles. As they rise, the particles of steam hit the blades of the turbine; even though one microscopic particle can only give it a microscopic push, the force of many tiny particles hitting the turbine can be enough to set it in motion.

31. D: The particles that make up the steam are not destroyed when they hit the turbine. Even though the particles are too small to see and they cannot be easily distinguished from the surrounding air, they still exist, and they do not suddenly change their nature—steam particles will not suddenly turn into

air or energy, and they certainly won't just disappear. Therefore, what most likely happens is just that they spread out and are scattered through the air.

32. D: The term for all the organisms of the same species in an ecosystem is a *population*. A *biome* is a kind of ecosystem (such as a tropical rain forest, desert, etc.), a *community* is a collective term for all the populations in an area, and a *habitat* is the environment in which an organism lives.

33. C: A cold, coniferous forest biome is called a *taiga*. Covering much of northern Asia and North America, taiga is actually the largest biome by area on Earth's land surface (not counting ocean biomes). An *ice cap* is a sheet of ice covering part of the Earth's surface; a *prairie* is a temperate, grassy biome such as much of the American Midwest; and a *tundra* is a cold, treeless biome characterized by frozen soil and lichen.

34. C: A healthy ecosystem has many different types of organism, interacting in a stable web of life.

35. D: The organisms in an ecosystem coexist in a balance that may have developed over long periods of time. A new species that didn't originally belong to the ecosystem might overuse resources needed by the other organisms in the ecosystem, or it may otherwise damage the ecosystem in unpredictable ways.

36. B: Anywhere near the Earth's surface, even at the peak of Mount Everest, the Earth's gravity pulls objects downward.

37. A: Plants are producers; they do not generally feed on other organisms, but they do produce energy from their environment. According to the description above, the organisms filling this role in the hydrothermal vent ecosystem are bacteria, which produce energy from the chemicals in their environment, making them producers as well. The copepods that feed on the bacteria are primary consumers, the snails and fish that feed on the copepods are secondary consumers, and the fungi that break down dead organisms are decomposers; none of these are producers, so they don't fill a similar niche to terrestrial plants.

Social Studies

1. B: Only the legislative branch has the power to declare war. The executive branch may ask the legislative branch to declare war, but the executive branch of itself cannot declare war. The judicial branch has nothing to do with the declaration of war. There is no federal branch of government.

2. C: The U.S. Constitution requires that a census be taken every 10 years. The other answer choices are either too low or too high.

3. B: A computer is a want instead of a need. Vegetables, medication, and education, however, could all be considered needs.

4. A: A group of islands is called an archipelago. An atoll is a coral reef that is ring shaped and surrounds a lagoon. An estuary is a body of brackish water near a coastline. An isthmus is a piece of land surrounded by water on two sides.

5. D: According to the U.S. Constitution, the electoral college makes the final decision in a presidential election. Based on the U.S. Constitution, the House of Representatives, the Senate, and the Supreme Court do not make the final decision in choosing a president.

6. B: A glacier is a large mass of slowly moving ice. A coral reef is an underwater colony of small animals. A fjord is narrow inlet found between two cliffs. A levee is a natural or man-made wall that controls water levels.

7. A: New York State was founded by the Dutch and therefore was originally New Netherland. As its main city, New York City was then called New Amsterdam. Charles Town was the original name of Charleston, South Carolina. Fort Goede Hoop (or just Fort Hoop) was the original name of Hartford, Connecticut. Fort Christina was a settlement near what is now Wilmington, Delaware.

8. B: A visa is a travel document that is issued by a government when a person from another country wants to enter that country. In Adam's case, he is an American traveling to Brazil, so he will need a visa from the Brazilian government to enter. A credit card will allow Adam to make purchases in Brazil but will not necessarily allow him to enter Brazil. A passport, which is issued by the home country, allows Adam to return to the United States but does not guarantee him entrance into Brazil. A boarding pass only allows Adam to board the plane.

9. D: In his farewell address, George Washington cautioned the American people against the rise of political parties. He did not warn against elections, Congress, or democracy.

10. C: The money left over at the end of the year represents a surplus for Balfour Paper Company. Capital represents the funding needed to start the company and is not relevant here (as Balfour Paper Company is clearly already up and running). Production represents the activity that occurs in the company. A deficit is a lack of funding and not an excess.

11. B: A forest is a natural resource. A factory and a flute are man-made resources. Friendship is a human quality but is not counted amongst resources, natural or man-made.

12. A: James Madison, John Adams, and James Monroe were all presidents. That leaves only John Jay, who was not president but was the first chief justice of the Supreme Court.

13. D: As indicated in the answer for question 10, capital is the money that Harmon needs to get his business off the ground. The budget is what Harmon will need to manage the money, but he cannot establish a budget without some money to begin with. Assets represent anything, tangible or intangible, that add value to an organization; the money, once received, will become an asset, but *asset* is not the correct term for the start-up funding. Debt is what Harmon wants to avoid because it would mean he owes more money than he has.

14. D: John Paul Jones announced, "I have not yet begun to fight!" when encouraged by the British to surrender. The other men did not make this statement. Patrick Henry is remembered primarily for stating, "Give me liberty or give me death!"

15. B: According to the map, the southernmost city is New York City. Jamestown, Newburgh, and White Plains are all north of New York City.

16. A: Lake Champlain lies directly to the east of New York in the northern corner of the state. Lake Ontario and Lake Erie lie to the west. The Finger Lakes are within the state.

17. C: The star that indicates a capital sits next to the city of Albany. New York, Troy, and Rochester, while all important cities in their own right, are not the capital of New York State.

18. C: The Declaration of Independence was written in 1776 (and was released on July 4, 1776). The other answer choices are either too early or too late.

19. C: The Treaty of Paris ended the American Revolution. The Treaty of Brussels united Belgium, France, Luxembourg, the Netherlands, and the United Kingdom against the post-World War II threat of Communism. The Treaty of Breslau ended the First Silesian War. There was no Treaty of Yorktown, although the Battle of Yorktown is considered one of the final battles of the American Revolution.

20. B: The number 2 indicates the Atlantic Ocean, which lies between the Eastern Hemisphere and the Western Hemisphere. The number 1 indicates the Pacific Ocean. The number 3 indicates the Arctic Ocean. There is no number on the map that indicates the Indian Ocean.

21. C: The number 3 indicates the Arctic Ocean. The number 1 indicates the Pacific Ocean, and the number 2 indicates the Atlantic Ocean. There is no number 4 on the map.

22. B: Africa lies to the east of South America and is indicated by the letter B: The letter A, indicating Greenland, is to the north of South America. The letters C and D, indicating Australia and Asia, respectively, both lie to the east of South America, but only Africa lies directly east.

23. D: Deep River will pay for road repairs with tax money collected from citizens. Assets represent anything, tangible or intangible, that add value to an organization; the money that Deep River receives becomes part of its assets, but *assets* is a broad term and does not indicate specifically how the city will select money. Typically, the money for road repairs comes from taxes. Inflation is a rise in prices resulting from a devaluing of money. Bartering is a type of trading.

24. B: Lava is the molten rock produced by an erupting volcano. Quartz, granite, and shoal are all types of rock, but none of them are volcanic.

25. C: There are 27 ratified amendments to the U.S. Constitution. The rest of the answer choices are either too high or too low. (There are 33 amendments that Congress has approved but only 27 have been ratified.)

26. C: At least 75 percent of the states must ratify an amendment to the U.S. Constitution before it can become law. The other answer choices are either too low or too high.

27. D: Factories are not natural resources, so they would not be monitored by the Department of Natural Resources. The lakes, fish, and wetlands, however, as natural resources, would be monitored by that department.

28. B: Jefferson Davis was president of the Confederacy during the Civil War. Robert E. Lee was a general in the Confederate Army. James Buchanan was the president of the United States prior to the Civil War. William T. Sherman was a general in the U.S. Army during the Civil War.

29. C: The right of women to vote is guaranteed by the 19th amendment, but not within the Bill of Rights. The Bill of Rights does grant the right to free speech, the right to practice religion, and the right to free press.

30. D: Everest is the highest mountain in the world. Kilimanjaro, Matterhorn, and Etna are all high peaks, but none of them is considered higher than Everest.

31. A: The Battle of Fort Sumter began the Civil War. Bull Run, Shiloh, and Camp Allegheny were all battles, but none of these battles began the Civil War.

32. C: Sequoia was a member of the Cherokee Nation and is known for inventing the Cherokee alphabet. Sequoia played no role in the languages of the Sioux, Apache, or Dakota nations.

33. B: Africa spans both the Northern Hemisphere and the Southern Hemisphere. Asia and Europe are entirely in the Northern Hemisphere. Australia is entirely in the Southern Hemisphere.

34. B: The abolitionists fought to end slavery. Protectionism and sectionalism were both movements during the Civil War but were not specifically focused on the goal to end slavery. Secessionists were fighting for the southern states to leave the United States.

35. C: To run for president, an individual must be at least 35 years of age. The other answer choices are either too low to too high.

36. B: To vote in an election, an individual must be at least 18 years of age. The other answer choices are either too low or too high.

37. A: Rosa Parks is remembered for refusing to move from her seat on the bus. Phyllis Wheatley was an African-American poet prior to the American Revolution. Harriet Tubman and Sojourner Truth were both abolitionists during the Civil War.

Vocabulary

1. D: something basic

2. C: go back

3. A: hard at work

4. C: nonsensical

5. C: requiring immediate action

6. B: burn

7. A: pay

8. D: faulty

9. B: unwilling

10. C: permission

11. B: sad

12. B: go downhill

13. B: turn up

14. A: inactive

15. B: sign up

16. C: dark and dirty

17. A: rebellion

18. C: out of date

19. B: exact copy

20. C: being safe from danger

21. D: short walk

22. A: important

23. B: top

24. B: close but not exact

25. D: follow

26. D: important paper

27. C: keep going

28. A: rival

29. B: make tired

30. C: eager to fight

31. A: leave out

32. B: weakened

33. C: poor farmers

34. A: journey to learn things

35. A: relaxed

36. C: bothersome pest

37. D: very happy

Spelling

1. *squonder* – this should be *squander*

2. *retreve* – this should be *retrieve*

3. *egzample* – this should be *example*

4. *swetter* – this should be *sweater*

5. *librery* – this should be *library*

6. *divedend* – this should be *dividend*

7. *lether* – this should be *leather*

8. *colum* – this should be *column*

9. *obblong* – this should be *oblong*

10. *incist* – this should be *insist*

11. *feeture* – this should be *feature*

12. *nesesary* – this should be *necessary*

13. *oxyjen* – this should be *oxygen*

14. *asimilate* – this should be *assimilate*

15. *fijet* – this should be *fidget*

16. *ubstruct* – this should be *obstruct*

17. *mithology* – this should be *mythology*

18. *ficility* – this should be *facility*

19. *alltho* – this should be *although*

20. *icycle* – this should be *icicle*

21. *domanant* – this should be *dominant*

22. *solow* – this should be *solo*

23. *fatige* – this should be *fatigue*

24. *increese* – this should be *increase*

25. NO MISTAKES

26. *curtin* – this should be *curtain*

27. *valyew* – this should be *value*

28. *colunny* – this should be *colony*

29. *imperor* – this should be *emperor*

30. *pateet* – this should be *petite*

Capitalization

1. A: a Sleepover should be a sleepover

2. C: friday Night should be Friday night

3. D: NO MISTAKES

4. A: "She will, i am should be "She will, I am

5. B: school Holiday should be school holiday

6. D: NO MISTAKES

7. B: judge Johnson, should be Judge Johnson,

8. C: one Direction should be One Direction

9. B: reverend Brown, came should be Reverend Brown, came

10. C: star wars movie should be Star Wars movie

11. B: "you should take should be "You should take

12. C: last Day of the Year should be last day of the year

13. B: kroger is opening a should be Kroger is opening a

14. C: by Extraterrestrials should be by extraterrestrials

15. B: battle hymn of should be Battle Hymn of

16. B: date easter falls should be date Easter falls

17. B: is the best Elementary School should be is the best elementary school

18. B: play Video Games after should be play video games after

19. B: a new nintendo should be a new Nintendo

20. A: Dad said uncle Bob should be Dad said Uncle Bob

21. C: and new York should be and New York

22. C: Doctor's Office should be doctor's office.

23. B: a Roast Beef dinner should be a roast beef dinner

24. C: philosopher's stone should be Philosopher's Stone

Punctuation

Ending Punctuation
1. Question mark (?)
2. Period (.)
3. Period (.)
4. Exclamation point (!)
5. Question mark (?)
6. Exclamation point (!)
7. Question mark (?)
8. Period (.)
9. Question mark (?)
10. Exclamation point (!)

Commas

1. In Houston, Texas, there is a huge rodeo in February.
2. Johnny said, "Let's go play on the swings."
3. It's going to rain today, isn't it?
4. Nate had three apples, two oranges, and a banana in his lunch box.
5. Eureka, a show on the SyFy channel, is about a town of geniuses.
6. The Revolutionary War officially ended on May 12, 1784.
7. Yes, thank you, I would love some cake.
8. Along with his friends, Evan thought he could help others.
9. Because of the lightning, we could not play outside.
10. We can vacation at the beach, or we can go to the city.
11. & 12. Answers will vary

Titles
1. <u>To Kill A Mockingbird</u> is my favorite novel.
2. The headline read, "Man Kills Seven in Subway."
3. My class went to see "An Ideal Husband," a play by Oscar Wilde.
4. <u>The Avengers</u> was the best movie this summer!
5. "What Sarah Said," by Death Cab for Cutie, is the best song ever.

Success Strategies

The most important thing you can do is to ignore your fears and jump into the test immediately. Do not be overwhelmed by any strange-sounding terms. You have to jump into the test like jumping into a pool—all at once is the easiest way.

Make Predictions

As you read and understand the question, try to guess what the answer will be. Remember that several of the answer choices are wrong, and once you begin reading them, your mind will immediately become cluttered with answer choices designed to throw you off. Your mind is typically the most focused immediately after you have read the question and digested its contents. If you can, try to predict what the correct answer will be. You may be surprised at what you can predict.

Quickly scan the choices and see if your prediction is in the listed answer choices. If it is, then you can be quite confident that you have the right answer. It still won't hurt to check the other answer choices, but most of the time, you've got it!

Answer the Question

It may seem obvious to only pick answer choices that answer the question, but the test writers can create some excellent answer choices that are wrong. Don't pick an answer just because it sounds right, or you believe it to be true. It MUST answer the question. Once you've made your selection, always go back and check it against the question and make sure that you didn't misread the question and that the answer choice does answer the question posed.

Benchmark

After you read the first answer choice, decide if you think it sounds correct or not. If it doesn't, move on to the next answer choice. If it does, mentally mark that answer choice. This doesn't mean that you've definitely selected it as your answer choice, it just means that it's the best you've seen thus far. Go ahead and read the next choice. If the next choice is worse than the one you've already selected, keep going to the next answer choice. If the next choice is better than the choice you've already selected, mentally mark the new answer choice as your best guess.

The first answer choice that you select becomes your standard. Every other answer choice must be benchmarked against that standard. That choice is correct until proven otherwise by another answer choice beating it out. Once you've decided that no other answer choice seems as good, do one final check to ensure that your answer choice answers the question posed.

Valid Information

Don't discount any of the information provided in the question. Every piece of information may be necessary to determine the correct answer. None of the information in the question is there to throw you off (while the answer choices will certainly have information to throw you off). If two seemingly unrelated topics are discussed, don't ignore either. You can be confident there is a relationship, or it wouldn't be included in the question, and you are probably going to have to determine what is that relationship to find the answer.

Avoid "Fact Traps"

Don't get distracted by a choice that is factually true. Your search is for the answer that answers the question. Stay focused and don't fall for an answer that is true but irrelevant. Always go back to the question and make sure you're choosing an answer that actually answers the question and is not just a true statement. An answer can be factually correct, but it MUST answer the question asked. Additionally, two answers can both be seemingly correct, so be sure to read all of the answer choices, and make sure that you get the one that BEST answers the question.

Milk the Question

Some of the questions may throw you completely off. They might deal with a subject you have not been exposed to, or one that you haven't reviewed in years. While your lack of knowledge about the subject will be a hindrance, the question itself can give you many clues that will help you find the correct answer. Read the question carefully and look for clues. Watch particularly for adjectives and nouns describing difficult terms or words that you don't recognize. Regardless of whether you completely understand a word or not, replacing it with a synonym, either provided or one you more familiar with, may help you to understand what the questions are asking. Rather than wracking your mind about specific detailed information concerning a difficult term or word, try to use mental substitutes that are easier to understand.

The Trap of Familiarity

Don't just choose a word because you recognize it. On difficult questions, you may not recognize a number of words in the answer choices. The test writers don't put "make-believe" words on the test, so don't think that just because you only recognize all the words in one answer choice that that answer choice must be correct. If you only recognize words in one answer choice, then focus on that one. Is it correct? Try your best to determine if it is correct. If it is, that's great. If not, eliminate it. Each word and answer choice you eliminate increases your chances of getting the question correct, even if you then have to guess among the unfamiliar choices.

Eliminate Answers

Eliminate choices as soon as you realize they are wrong. But be careful! Make sure you consider all of the possible answer choices. Just because one appears right, doesn't mean that the next one won't be even better! The test writers will usually put more than one good answer choice for every question, so read all of them. Don't worry if you are stuck between two that seem right. By getting down to just two remaining possible choices, your odds are now 50/50. Rather than wasting too much time, play the odds. You are guessing, but guessing wisely because you've been able to knock out some of the answer choices that you know are wrong. If you are eliminating choices and realize that the last answer choice you are left with is also obviously wrong, don't panic. Start over and consider each choice again. There may easily be something that you missed the first time and will realize on the second pass.

Tough Questions

If you are stumped on a problem or it appears too hard or too difficult, don't waste time. Move on! Remember though, if you can quickly check for obviously incorrect answer choices, your chances of guessing correctly are greatly improved. Before you completely give up, at least try to knock out a couple of possible answers. Eliminate what you can and then guess at the remaining answer choices before moving on.

Brainstorm

If you get stuck on a difficult question, spend a few seconds quickly brainstorming. Run through the complete list of possible answer choices. Look at each choice and ask yourself, "Could this answer the question satisfactorily?" Go through each answer choice and consider it independently of the others. By systematically going through all possibilities, you may find something that you would otherwise overlook. Remember though that when you get stuck, it's important to try to keep moving.

Read Carefully

Understand the problem. Read the question and answer choices carefully. Don't miss the question because you misread the terms. You have plenty of time to read each question thoroughly and make sure you understand what is being asked. Yet a happy medium must be attained, so don't waste too much time. You must read carefully, but efficiently.

Face Value

When in doubt, use common sense. Always accept the situation in the problem at face value. Don't read too much into it. These problems will not require you to make huge leaps of logic. The test writers aren't trying to throw you off with a cheap trick. If you have to go beyond creativity and make a leap of logic in order to have an answer choice answer the question, then you should look at the other answer choices. Don't overcomplicate the problem by creating theoretical relationships or explanations that will warp time or space. These are normal problems rooted in reality. It's just that the applicable relationship or explanation may not be readily apparent and you have to figure things out. Use your common sense to interpret anything that isn't clear.

Prefixes

If you're having trouble with a word in the question or answer choices, try dissecting it. Take advantage of every clue that the word might include. Prefixes and suffixes can be a huge help. Usually they allow you to determine a basic meaning. Pre- means before, post- means after, pro - is positive, de- is negative. From these prefixes and suffixes, you can get an idea of the general meaning of the word and try to put it into context. Beware though of any traps. Just because con- is the opposite of pro-, doesn't necessarily mean congress is the opposite of progress!

Hedge Phrases

Watch out for critical hedge phrases, led off with words such as "likely," "may," "can," "sometimes," "often," "almost," "mostly," "usually," "generally," "rarely," and "sometimes." Question writers insert these hedge phrases to cover every possibility. Often an answer choice will be wrong simply because it leaves no room for exception. Unless the situation calls for them, avoid answer choices that have definitive words like "exactly," and "always."

Switchback Words

Stay alert for "switchbacks." These are the words and phrases frequently used to alert you to shifts in thought. The most common switchback word is "but." Others include "although," "however," "nevertheless," "on the other hand," "even though," "while," "in spite of," "despite," and "regardless of."

New Information

Correct answer choices will rarely have completely new information included. Answer choices typically are straightforward reflections of the material asked about and will directly relate to the question. If a new piece of information is included in an answer choice that doesn't even seem to relate to the topic being asked about, then that answer choice is likely incorrect. All of the information needed to answer the question is usually provided for you in the question. You should not have to make guesses that are unsupported or choose answer choices that require unknown information that cannot be reasoned from what is given.

Time Management

On technical questions, don't get lost on the technical terms. Don't spend too much time on any one question. If you don't know what a term means, then odds are you aren't going to get much further since you don't have a dictionary. You should be able to immediately recognize whether or not you know a term. If you don't, work with the other clues that you have—the other answer choices and terms provided—but don't waste too much time trying to figure out a difficult term that you don't know.

Contextual Clues

Look for contextual clues. An answer can be right but not the correct answer. The contextual clues will help you find the answer that is most right and is correct. Understand the context in which a phrase or statement is made. This will help you make important distinctions.

Don't Panic

Panicking will not answer any questions for you; therefore, it isn't helpful. When you first see the question, if your mind goes blank, take a deep breath. Force yourself to mechanically go through the steps of solving the problem using the strategies you've learned.

Pace Yourself

Don't get clock fever. It's easy to be overwhelmed when you're looking at a page full of questions, your mind is full of random thoughts and feeling confused, and the clock is ticking down faster than you would like. Calm down and maintain the pace that you have set for yourself. As long as you are on track by monitoring your pace, you are guaranteed to have enough time for yourself. When you get to the last few minutes of the test, it may seem like you won't have enough time left, but if you only have as many questions as you should have left at that point, then you're right on track!

Answer Selection

The best way to pick an answer choice is to eliminate all of those that are wrong, until only one is left and confirm that is the correct answer. Sometimes though, an answer choice may immediately look right. Be careful! Take a second to make sure that the other choices are not equally obvious. Don't make a hasty mistake. There are only two times that you should stop before checking other answers. First is when you are positive that the answer choice you have selected is correct. Second is when time is almost out and you have to make a quick guess!

Check Your Work

Since you will probably not know every term listed and the answer to every question, it is important that you get credit for the ones that you do know. Don't miss any questions through careless mistakes. If at all possible, try to take a second to look back over your answer selection and make sure you've selected the correct answer choice and haven't made a costly careless mistake (such as marking an answer choice that you didn't mean to mark). The time it takes for this quick double check should more than pay for itself in caught mistakes.

Beware of Directly Quoted Answers

Sometimes an answer choice will repeat word for word a portion of the question or reference section. However, beware of such exact duplication. It may be a trap! More than likely, the correct choice will paraphrase or summarize a point, rather than being exactly the same wording.

Slang

Scientific sounding answers are better than slang ones. An answer choice that begins "To compare the outcomes..." is much more likely to be correct than one that begins "Because some people insisted..."

Extreme Statements

Avoid wild answers that throw out highly controversial ideas that are proclaimed as established fact. An answer choice that states the "process should used in certain situations, if..." is much more likely to be correct than one that states the "process should be discontinued completely." The first is a calm rational statement and doesn't even make a definitive, uncompromising stance, using a hedge word "if" to provide wiggle room, whereas the second choice is a radical idea and far more extreme.

Answer Choice Families

When you have two or more answer choices that are direct opposites or parallels, one of them is usually the correct answer. For instance, if one answer choice states "x increases" and another answer choice states "x decreases" or "y increases," then those two or three answer choices are very similar in construction and fall into the same family of answer choices. A family of answer choices consists of two or three answer choices, very similar in construction, but often with directly opposite meanings. Usually the correct answer choice will be in that family of answer choices. The "odd man out" or answer choice that doesn't seem to fit the parallel construction of the other answer choices is more likely to be incorrect.

How to Overcome Test Anxiety

The very nature of tests caters to some level of anxiety, nervousness, or tension, just as we feel for any important event that occurs in our lives. A little bit of anxiety or nervousness can be a good thing. It helps us with motivation, and makes achievement just that much sweeter. However, too much anxiety can be a problem, especially if it hinders our ability to function and perform.

"Test anxiety," is the term that refers to the emotional reactions that some test-takers experience when faced with a test or exam. Having a fear of testing and exams is based upon a rational fear, since the test-taker's performance can shape the course of an academic career. Nevertheless, experiencing excessive fear of examinations will only interfere with the test-taker's ability to perform and chance to be successful.

There are a large variety of causes that can contribute to the development and sensation of test anxiety. These include, but are not limited to, lack of preparation and worrying about issues surrounding the test.

Lack of Preparation

Lack of preparation can be identified by the following behaviors or situations:

Not scheduling enough time to study, and therefore cramming the night before the test or exam
Managing time poorly, to create the sensation that there is not enough time to do everything
Failing to organize the text information in advance, so that the study material consists of the entire text and not simply the pertinent information
Poor overall studying habits

Worrying, on the other hand, can be related to both the test taker, or many other factors around him/her that will be affected by the results of the test. These include worrying about:

Previous performances on similar exams, or exams in general
How friends and other students are achieving
The negative consequences that will result from a poor grade or failure

There are three primary elements to test anxiety. Physical components, which involve the same typical bodily reactions as those to acute anxiety (to be discussed below). Emotional factors have to do with fear or panic. Mental or cognitive issues concerning attention spans and memory abilities.

Physical Signals

There are many different symptoms of test anxiety, and these are not limited to mental and emotional strain. Frequently there are a range of physical signals that will let a test taker know that he/she is suffering from test anxiety. These bodily changes can include the following:

Perspiring
Sweaty palms
Wet, trembling hands
Nausea
Dry mouth
A knot in the stomach
Headache
Faintness
Muscle tension
Aching shoulders, back and neck
Rapid heart beat
Feeling too hot/cold

To recognize the sensation of test anxiety, a test-taker should monitor him/herself for the following sensations:

The physical distress symptoms as listed above
Emotional sensitivity, expressing emotional feelings such as the need to cry or laugh too much, or a sensation of anger or helplessness
A decreased ability to think, causing the test-taker to blank out or have racing thoughts that are hard to organize or control.

Though most students will feel some level of anxiety when faced with a test or exam, the majority can cope with that anxiety and maintain it at a manageable level. However, those who cannot are faced with a very real and very serious condition, which can and should be controlled for the immeasurable benefit of this sufferer.

Naturally, these sensations lead to negative results for the testing experience. The most common effects of test anxiety have to do with nervousness and mental blocking.

Nervousness

Nervousness can appear in several different levels:

The test-taker's difficulty, or even inability to read and understand the questions on the test
The difficulty or inability to organize thoughts to a coherent form
The difficulty or inability to recall key words and concepts relating to the testing questions (especially essays)
The receipt of poor grades on a test, though the test material was well known by the test taker

Conversely, a person may also experience mental blocking, which involves:

Blanking out on test questions
Only remembering the correct answers to the questions when the test has already finished.

Fortunately for test anxiety sufferers, beating these feelings, to a large degree, has to do with proper preparation. When a test taker has a feeling of preparedness, then anxiety will be dramatically lessened.

The first step to resolving anxiety issues is to distinguish which of the two types of anxiety are being suffered. If the anxiety is a direct result of a lack of preparation, this should be considered a normal reaction, and the anxiety level (as opposed to the test results) shouldn't be anything to worry about. However, if, when adequately prepared, the test-taker still panics, blanks out, or seems to overreact, this is not a fully rational reaction. While this can be considered normal too, there are many ways to combat and overcome these effects.

Remember that anxiety cannot be entirely eliminated, however, there are ways to minimize it, to make the anxiety easier to manage. Preparation is one of the best ways to minimize test anxiety. Therefore the following techniques are wise in order to best fight off any anxiety that may want to build.

To begin with, try to avoid cramming before a test, whenever it is possible. By trying to memorize an entire term's worth of information in one day, you'll be shocking your system, and not giving yourself a very good chance to absorb the information. This is an easy path to anxiety, so for those who suffer from test anxiety, cramming should not even be considered an option.

Instead of cramming, work throughout the semester to combine all of the material which is presented throughout the semester, and work on it gradually as the course goes by, making sure to master the main concepts first, leaving minor details for a week or so before the test.

To study for the upcoming exam, be sure to pose questions that may be on the examination, to gauge the ability to answer them by integrating the ideas from your texts, notes and lectures, as well as any supplementary readings.

If it is truly impossible to cover all of the information that was covered in that particular term, concentrate on the most important portions, that can be covered very well. Learn these concepts as best as possible, so that when the test comes, a goal can be made to use these concepts as presentations of your knowledge.

In addition to study habits, changes in attitude are critical to beating a struggle with test anxiety. In fact, an improvement of the perspective over the entire test-taking experience can actually help a test taker to enjoy studying and therefore improve the overall experience. Be certain not to overemphasize the significance of the grade - know that the result of the test is neither a reflection of self worth, nor is it a measure of intelligence; one grade will not predict a person's future success.

To improve an overall testing outlook, the following steps should be tried:

Keeping in mind that the most reasonable expectation for taking a test is to expect to try to demonstrate as much of what you know as you possibly can. Reminding ourselves that a test is only one test; this is not the only one, and there will be others.
The thought of thinking of oneself in an irrational, all-or-nothing term should be avoided at all costs.
A reward should be designated for after the test, so there's something to look forward to. Whether it be going to a movie, going out to eat, or simply visiting friends, schedule it in advance, and do it no matter what result is expected on the exam.

Test-takers should also keep in mind that the basics are some of the most important things, even beyond anti-anxiety techniques and studying. Never neglect the basic social, emotional and biological needs, in order to try to absorb information. In order to best achieve, these three factors must be held as just as important as the studying itself.

Study Steps

Remember the following important steps for studying:

Maintain healthy nutrition and exercise habits. Continue both your recreational activities and social pass times. These both contribute to your physical and emotional well being.
Be certain to get a good amount of sleep, especially the night before the test, because when you're overtired you are not able to perform to the best of your best ability.
Keep the studying pace to a moderate level by taking breaks when they are needed, and varying the work whenever possible, to keep the mind fresh instead of getting bored.
When enough studying has been done that all the material that can be learned has been learned, and the test taker is prepared for the test, stop studying and do something relaxing such as listening to music, watching a movie, or taking a warm bubble bath.

There are also many other techniques to minimize the uneasiness or apprehension that is experienced along with test anxiety before, during, or even after the examination. In fact, there are a great deal of things that can be done to stop anxiety from interfering with lifestyle and performance. Again, remember that anxiety will not be eliminated entirely, and it shouldn't be. Otherwise that "up" feeling for exams would not exist, and most of us depend on that sensation to perform better than usual. However, this anxiety has to be at a level that is manageable.

Of course, as we have just discussed, being prepared for the exam is half the battle right away. Attending all classes, finding out what knowledge will be expected on the exam, and knowing the exam schedules are easy steps to lowering anxiety. Keeping up with work will remove the need to cram, and efficient study habits will eliminate wasted time. Studying should be done in an ideal location for concentration, so that it is simple to become interested in the material and give it complete attention. A method such as SQ3R (Survey, Question, Read, Recite, Review) is a wonderful key to follow to make sure that the study habits are as effective as possible, especially in the case of learning from a textbook. Flashcards are great techniques for memorization. Learning to take good notes will mean that notes will be full of useful information, so that less sifting will need to be done to seek out what is pertinent for studying. Reviewing notes after class and then again on occasion will keep the information fresh in the mind. From notes that have been taken summary sheets and outlines can be made for simpler reviewing.

A study group can also be a very motivational and helpful place to study, as there will be a sharing of ideas, all of the minds can work together, to make sure that everyone understands, and the studying will be made more interesting because it will be a social occasion.

Basically, though, as long as the test-taker remains organized and self confident, with efficient study habits, less time will need to be spent studying, and higher grades will be achieved.

To become self confident, there are many useful steps. The first of these is "self talk." It has been shown through extensive research, that self-talk for students who suffer from test anxiety, should be well monitored, in order to make sure that it contributes to self confidence as opposed to sinking the student. Frequently the self talk of test-anxious students is negative or self-defeating, thinking that everyone else is smarter and faster, that they always mess up, and that if they don't do well, they'll fail the entire course. It is important to decreasing anxiety that awareness is made of self talk. Try writing any negative self thoughts and then disputing them with a positive statement instead. Begin self-encouragement as though it was a friend speaking. Repeat positive statements to help reprogram the mind to believing in successes instead of failures.

Helpful Techniques

Other extremely helpful techniques include:

Self-visualization of doing well and reaching goals
While aiming for an "A" level of understanding, don't try to "overprotect" by setting your expectations lower. This will only convince the mind to stop studying in order to meet the lower expectations.
Don't make comparisons with the results or habits of other students. These are individual factors, and different things work for different people, causing different results.
Strive to become an expert in learning what works well, and what can be done in order to improve. Consider collecting this data in a journal.

Create rewards for after studying instead of doing things before studying that will only turn into avoidance behaviors.

Make a practice of relaxing - by using methods such as progressive relaxation, self-hypnosis, guided imagery, etc - in order to make relaxation an automatic sensation.

Work on creating a state of relaxed concentration so that concentrating will take on the focus of the mind, so that none will be wasted on worrying.

Take good care of the physical self by eating well and getting enough sleep. Plan in time for exercise and stick to this plan.

Beyond these techniques, there are other methods to be used before, during and after the test that will help the test-taker perform well in addition to overcoming anxiety.

Before the exam comes the academic preparation. This involves establishing a study schedule and beginning at least one week before the actual date of the test. By doing this, the anxiety of not having enough time to study for the test will be automatically eliminated. Moreover, this will make the studying a much more effective experience, ensuring that the learning will be an easier process. This relieves much undue pressure on the test-taker.

Summary sheets, note cards, and flash cards with the main concepts and examples of these main concepts should be prepared in advance of the actual studying time. A topic should never be eliminated from this process. By omitting a topic because it isn't expected to be on the test is only setting up the test-taker for anxiety should it actually appear on the exam. Utilize the course syllabus for laying out the topics that should be studied. Carefully go over the notes that were made in class, paying special attention to any of the issues that the professor took special care to emphasize while lecturing in class. In the textbooks, use the chapter review, or if possible, the chapter tests, to begin your review.

It may even be possible to ask the instructor what information will be covered on the exam, or what the format of the exam will be (for example, multiple choice, essay, free form, true-false). Additionally, see if it is possible to find out how many questions will be on the test. If a review sheet or sample test has been offered by the professor, make good use of it, above anything else, for the preparation for the test. Another great resource for getting to know the examination is reviewing tests from previous semesters. Use these tests to review, and aim to achieve a 100% score on each of the possible topics. With a few exceptions, the goal that you set for yourself is the highest one that you will reach.

Take all of the questions that were assigned as homework, and rework them to any other possible course material. The more problems reworked, the more skill and confidence will form as a result. When forming the solution to a problem, write out each of the steps. Don't simply do head work. By doing as many steps on paper as possible, much clarification and therefore confidence will be formed. Do this with as many homework problems as possible, before checking the answers. By checking the answer after each problem, a reinforcement will exist, that will not be on the exam. Study situations should be as exam-like as possible, to prime the test-taker's system for the experience. By waiting to check the answers at the end, a psychological advantage will be formed, to decrease the stress factor.

Another fantastic reason for not cramming is the avoidance of confusion in concepts, especially when it comes to mathematics. 8-10 hours of study will become one hundred percent more effective if it is spread out over a week or at least several days, instead of doing it all in one sitting. Recognize that the human brain requires time in order to assimilate new material, so frequent breaks and a span of study time over several days will be much more beneficial.

Additionally, don't study right up until the point of the exam. Studying should stop a minimum of one hour before the exam begins. This allows the brain to rest and put things in their proper order. This will also provide the time to become as relaxed as possible when going into the examination room. The test-taker will also have time to eat well and eat sensibly. Know that the brain needs food as much as the rest of the body. With enough food and enough sleep, as well as a relaxed attitude, the body and the mind are primed for success.

Avoid any anxious classmates who are talking about the exam. These students only spread anxiety, and are not worth sharing the anxious sentimentalities.

Before the test also involves creating a positive attitude, so mental preparation should also be a point of concentration. There are many keys to creating a positive attitude. Should fears become rushing in, make a visualization of taking the exam, doing well, and seeing an A written on the paper. Write out a list of affirmations that will bring a feeling of confidence, such as "I am doing well in my English class," "I studied well and know my material," "I enjoy this class." Even if the affirmations aren't believed at first, it sends a positive message to the subconscious which will result in an alteration of the overall belief system, which is the system that creates reality.

If a sensation of panic begins, work with the fear and imagine the very worst! Work through the entire scenario of not passing the test, failing the entire course, and dropping out of school, followed by not getting a job, and pushing a shopping cart through the dark alley where you'll live. This will place things into perspective! Then, practice deep breathing and create a visualization of the opposite situation - achieving an "A" on the exam, passing the entire course, receiving the degree at a graduation ceremony.

On the day of the test, there are many things to be done to ensure the best results, as well as the most calm outlook. The following stages are suggested in order to maximize test-taking potential:

Begin the examination day with a moderate breakfast, and avoid any coffee or beverages with caffeine if the test taker is prone to jitters. Even people who are used to managing caffeine can feel jittery or light-headed when it is taken on a test day.

Attempt to do something that is relaxing before the examination begins. As last minute cramming clouds the mastering of overall concepts, it is better to use this time to create a calming outlook.

Be certain to arrive at the test location well in advance, in order to provide time to select a location that is away from doors, windows and other distractions, as well as giving enough time to relax before the test begins.

Keep away from anxiety generating classmates who will upset the sensation of stability and relaxation that is being attempted before the exam.

Should the waiting period before the exam begins cause anxiety, create a self-distraction by reading a light magazine or something else that is relaxing and simple.

During the exam itself, read the entire exam from beginning to end, and find out how much time should be allotted to each individual problem. Once writing the exam, should more time be taken for a problem, it should be abandoned, in order to begin another problem. If there is time at the end, the unfinished problem can always be returned to and completed.

Read the instructions very carefully - twice - so that unpleasant surprises won't follow during or after the exam has ended.

When writing the exam, pretend that the situation is actually simply the completion of homework within a library, or at home. This will assist in forming a relaxed atmosphere, and will allow the brain extra focus for the complex thinking function.

Begin the exam with all of the questions with which the most confidence is felt. This will build the confidence level regarding the entire exam and will begin a quality momentum. This will also create encouragement for trying the problems where uncertainty resides.

Going with the "gut instinct" is always the way to go when solving a problem. Second guessing should be avoided at all costs. Have confidence in the ability to do well.

For essay questions, create an outline in advance that will keep the mind organized and make certain that all of the points are remembered. For multiple choice, read every answer, even if the correct one has been spotted - a better one may exist.

Continue at a pace that is reasonable and not rushed, in order to be able to work carefully. Provide enough time to go over the answers at the end, to check for small errors that can be corrected.

Should a feeling of panic begin, breathe deeply, and think of the feeling of the body releasing sand through its pores. Visualize a calm, peaceful place, and include all of the sights, sounds and sensations of this image. Continue the deep breathing, and take a few minutes to continue this with closed eyes. When all is well again, return to the test.

If a "blanking" occurs for a certain question, skip it and move on to the next question. There will be time to return to the other question later. Get everything done that can be done, first, to guarantee all the grades that can be compiled, and to build all of the confidence possible. Then return to the weaker questions to build the marks from there.

Remember, one's own reality can be created, so as long as the belief is there, success will follow. And remember: anxiety can happen later, right now, there's an exam to be written!

After the examination is complete, whether there is a feeling for a good grade or a bad grade, don't dwell on the exam, and be certain to follow through on the reward that was promised...and enjoy it! Don't dwell on any mistakes that have been made, as there is nothing that can be done at this point anyway.

Additionally, don't begin to study for the next test right away. Do something relaxing for a while, and let the mind relax and prepare itself to begin absorbing information again.

From the results of the exam - both the grade and the entire experience, be certain to learn from what has gone on. Perfect studying habits and work some more on confidence in order to make the next examination experience even better than the last one.

Learn to avoid places where openings occurred for laziness, procrastination and day dreaming.

Use the time between this exam and the next one to better learn to relax, even learning to relax on cue, so that any anxiety can be controlled during the next exam. Learn how to relax the body. Slouch in your chair if that helps. Tighten and then relax all of the different muscle groups, one group at a time, beginning with the feet and then working all the way up to the neck and face. This will ultimately relax the muscles more than they were to begin with. Learn how to breathe deeply and comfortably, and focus on this breathing going in and out as a relaxing thought. With every exhale, repeat the word "relax."

As common as test anxiety is, it is very possible to overcome it. Make yourself one of the test-takers who overcome this frustrating hindrance.

Additional Bonus Material

Due to our efforts to try to keep this book to a manageable length, we've created a link that will give you access to all of your additional bonus material.

Please visit http://www.mometrix.com/bonus948/itbsl11g5 to access the information.